Multinationals: Foreign Divestment and Disclosure

Multinationals: Foreign Divestment and Disclosure

Michael C. McDermott

Lecturer in International Business
The University of Strathclyde

McGRAW-HILL BOOK COMPANY

London · New York · St Louis · San Francisco · Auckland
Bogotá · Guatemala · Hamburg · Lisbon · Madrid · Mexico
Montreal · New Delhi · Panama · Paris · San Juan · São Paulo
Singapore · Sydney · Tokyo · Toronto

Published by
McGRAW-HILL Book Company (UK) Limited
MAIDENHEAD · BERKSHIRE · ENGLAND

British Library Cataloguing in Publication Data
McDermott, Michael C.
Multinationals: foreign divestment and disclosure
1. Multinational companies
I. Title
338.8'8841

ISBN 0-07-084198-5

Library of Congress Cataloging-in-Publication Data
McDermott, Michael C.
    Multinationals: foreign divestment and disclosure/
    Michael C. McDermott.
        p.   cm.
    Bibliography: p.
    Includes index.
    ISBN 0-07-084198-5
    1. Plant shutdowns—Great Britain.   2. Disinvestment—Great
Britain.   3. Employees, Reporting to—Great Britain.
4. International business enterprises—Great Britain.   I. Title.
HD5708.55.G7M37   1989
338.8'8841—dc 19   88-34875

1234 CUP 8909

Typeset by Advanced Filmsetters (Glasgow) Ltd, Glasgow
and printed and bound at the University Press, Cambridge.

To
Ann, Elizabeth-Anne, and Michael

Contents

Preface

This book is unique in that it offers a comprehensive review of large foreign divestments in four industries in one 'host' country (i.e. Britain). It features 14 closures, involving 11 named multinational corporations (MNCs) from five countries. Previous studies have focused on fewer closures and companies, and often the latter have been headquartered in the same country, and their identity has been disguised.

The case studies serve to reveal the main causes of these closures, and the response of the MNCs to a deteriorating business environment. They also illustrate the extent to which these corporations complied with their legal requirement to inform (and consult) employees. In addition, the book assesses the key 'Employment and industrial relations' section of the OECD's Guidelines for Multinational Enterprises.

During the early 1980s, when the European Commission was seeking to enhance employees' rights to more extensive information disclosure, especially by MNCs, it was argued that such legislation (i.e. the Vredeling Proposals) was unnecessary because MNCs already complied with the OECD Guidelines. The UK government was one of the main advocates of this view. It is, therefore, singly appropriate that any assessment of the OECD's Guidelines and/or the Vredeling Proposals should be based on UK evidence. The Vredeling debate has been rekindled by recent speeches by officials of the European Community who espouse the ideal of a 'United States of Europe', and by national leaders who are eager to protect 'national sovereignty'. This book contributes to that debate.

It also illustrates to corporate executives, employees' representatives and policy-makers the machinations involved in the foreign divestment process. The cases further reveal the potential pitfalls during the divestment process. They show that companies can minimize adverse publicity by thorough planning prior to implementing the divestment decision. Similarly, employees' representatives too may learn from their previous experiences.

Acknowledgements

The author extends his thanks to his former colleagues at the Department of Accounting and Finance at the University of Glasgow. A special mention is due to my doctoral supervisor, Professor S. J. Gray for his encouragement and guidance. Much of the work on this book has been done since I moved to the University of Strathclyde, and I am in debt to my students and colleagues in Strathclyde International Business Unit at the Department of Marketing for providing such a stimulating working environment.

In researching this book invaluable assistance was received from numerous individuals and organizations, but especially from past and present management and employees of many of the companies in the case studies (see Chapters 4–7).

The staff of McGraw-Hill have also been remarkably helpful, and I thank Julie Ganner, Liz Nemececk, and Sue Hughes for their advice and patience.

Finally, I would like to thank Betty McFarlane and Elizabeth McCairns for their secretarial assistance.

List of Abbreviations

ACAS   Advisory, Conciliation and Arbitration Service
AEU   Amalgamated Engineering Union
AUEW   Amalgamated Union of Engineering Workers. NB This is the same union as AEU—only its name has changed.
ATGWU   Amalgamated Transport and General Workers' Union
CIME   Committee on International Investment and Multinational Enterprises
CEO   chief executive officer
CPG   Consumer Products Group (Singer)
EC   European Community
EPA   Employment Protection Act
ETUC   European Trade Union Confederation
fdi   foreign direct investment
FPU   Forward Planning Unit (Singer)
ICEF   International Federation of Chemical, Energy and General Workers
ILO   International Labour Office
IPG   Industrial Products Group (Singer)
JCC   Joint Consultative Committee
LDCs   lesser developed countries
MNCs   multinational corporations
NCP   National Contact Point
NICs   newly industrializing countries
OECD   Organization for Economic Co-operation and Development
PLC   product life-cycle
PWAF   'Plant With a Future' (Caterpillar)
TUAC   Trades Union Advisory Committee
TUC   Trades Union Congress
TGWU   Transport and General Workers' Union
UAW   United Auto Workers

1
Introduction

Since 1945, the global economy has experienced distinct periods of economic growth and recession. The main watershed has been the 1973 oil crisis, which abruptly terminated almost thirty years of continuous growth. The subsequent slump, which lasted until the early 1980s, saw in many Western countries record levels of unemployment, severe cut-backs in manufacturing production, rapid inflation and record high interest rates in the postwar era. To make matters worse, international competition intensified in many sectors (e.g. automobiles, consumer electronics, and tyres), and producers from the Eastern bloc and the Far East achieved substantial import penetration.

But by about 1984, many companies in Europe and the USA had recovered from the difficulties of the previous ten years. Corporate weaknesses (e.g. low productivity, high costs, poor marketing) had been overcome in many companies, and the business environment had improved as inflation and interest rates had returned to more acceptable levels. After years of retrenchment, many companies regained their confidence and embarked on a new expansionist phase, marked by the boom in merger activity in Europe and the USA since 1984.[1]

As of the end of 1988, there is no evidence to suggest a slow-down in corporate expansionism. Indeed, the prospect of '1992' is acting as a powerful stimulus to cross-border expansion in Europe. Against such an expansionist climate of foreign direct *investment*, the publication of a book on foreign *divestment* may appear inappropriate. But, as is argued below, the main trends in international business during the second half of the 1980s may necessitate large-scale corporate restructuring and job losses in the final years of the twentieth century.

1.1 Foreign direct investment: a qualitative review

Never before have nations throughout the world competed so fiercely to attract foreign direct investment (fdi) by multinational corporations (MNCs). Until recently, a number of countries at various stages of economic development were sceptical of the benefits of inward investment. For example, in the 1970s Canada sought to restrict fdi, but it reversed this policy in 1985. Similarly, in Europe, since 1982 Portugal has welcomed fdi, while neighbouring Spain further relaxed its bureaucratic measures in 1985. With their labour cheap by European standards, and as members of the European Community (EC) since January 1986, both Iberian countries have emerged as yet further major bidders for internationally mobile investment projects that are looking for a base in the EC. They offer a highly favourable environment for potential investors, and foreign direct investment in these countries has grown dramatically in the 1980s. Their success in attracting such investment has serious implications for other EC countries hoping to win and maintain fdi projects.

In lesser developed countries (LDCs), too, fdi controls have been relaxed (e.g. China 1986, India 1988, Indonesia 1986, Venezuela 1986, and Vietnam 1988) or scrapped (e.g. the Andean Pact of 1970, which broke up in the early 1980s). The global auction to win fdi clearly benefits the MNCs, which can locate wherever they choose. Sometimes a MNC's plant location decision hinges mainly on whichever country provides the most generous financial incentives.

But why are countries so eager to attract foreign direct investment? After all, there have been celebrated cases in which the activities of MNCs have called forth stern criticism. Consider the illegal share support scheme of Guinness in its 1986 bid for Distillers; the marketing by Eli Lilley of Opren, a drug for arthritis which had serious side-effects; Hoffman La Roche's transfer pricing in the 1970s; ITT's political intervention in Chile in 1973; the Lockheed bribery scandal; Nestlé and the baby food scandal in the Third World; and the worst ever industrial disaster, at Union Carbide's Bhopal plant in 1984, which killed more than 2000 people. Indeed, some opponents of MNCs, the star performers of the capitalist system, and their activities have registered their protest by the most extreme action; the chairman of France's Renault and a top executive of Germany's Siemens have both been assassinated in politically inspired attacks.

While foreign direct investment may hold some costs for the host nation, most countries have concluded that these are outweighed by the benefits. Host nations hope to accelerate economic development by attracting such investment, and it is conspicuous that, of the LDCs, those that have been most successful in this regard have more impressive growth rates than other nations from the same region (e.g. in Latin America, Mexico v. Brazil; in the Far East, Singapore v. Malaysia).

Foreign direct investment benefits the host nation in innumerable ways. It can have a positive impact on labour and capital markets, and can generate foreign exchange, improve the balance of payments, transfer skills and technology, etc. This is why there is so much competitive bidding among nations to attract such investment, and as the cost of winning it increases, the net overall benefit to the host country must inevitably fall. Indeed, the EC has had to impose a ceiling on the level of financial incentives that countries can offer potential investors. Despite this, there have been several cases in which EC countries have accused each other of poaching jobs by offering illegal inducements. For example, in 1983 the UK government accused Timex and Linotype-Paul, which was a subsidiary of Allied Corporation, of accepting illegal incentives from the French and German governments, respectively. The UK government, on the other hand, was accused of offering illegal payments to persuade Hyster to transfer production from the Netherlands to the UK.[2]

In contrast to foreign direct investment, foreign divestment by plant closure has negative consequences for the host nation; it has an adverse effect on the labour market as jobs are lost, foreign exchange earnings may decline, the host nation's trade position may worsen, etc. However, the host nation that renders divestment difficult for the MNC is likely to succeed only in reducing its attractiveness to potential investors. Indeed, in addition to offering financial incentives, many host nations appear to be dismantling any controls that may be unattractive to inward investors; e.g. France has relaxed its labour laws.

Thus the 1980s have been a period of deregulation of fdi controls. More and more countries, even those that once shunned fdi, are competing to attract MNCs to their shores. Given that the focus of this book is foreign divestment in the UK, it is important to stress that the UK still remains a most popular location among foreign investors, and the favourite in Europe among US, Japanese and Korean investors. Its continued popularity may be seen as a tribute to the adaptability of its trade unions and workers. For example, in some regions with reputations for poor labour relations and union militancy, the largest employers include foreign MNCs which have either non-union plants, or single-union agreements. Clydeside, Scotland, has attracted IBM and more recently Compaq, while Tyneside in north-east England has Komatsu and Nissan of Japan, and Goldstar and Samsung of Korea. This pattern is being repeated in regions of other European countries (e.g. in Lorraine in France).

The late 1970s to early 1980s was a period in which market conditions forced many MNCs in mature and/or depressed industries to undertake a worldwide rationalization of their operations. Consequently, there was a high incidence of plant closures, including foreign-owned ones, throughout Europe and the USA. In the UK, the economies of both Scotland and north-east England, along with Northern Ireland and Wales, were badly hit by a number of foreign-owned plant closures.

Happily, the mid- to late 1980s have seen a sharp decline in large foreign-owned plant closures in Europe. Indeed, this period has seen an expansion of operations by MNCs, rather than a retrenchment. The main trends have been:

— the sharp increase in fdi by Japanese companies;
— the emergence of fdi from the newly industrializing countries (NICs), such as South Korea and Taiwan;
— the boom in international takeovers, owing especially to European MNCs buying market shares in the USA and preparing for '1992' at home.

In the short term, these investment flows are likely to continue, but in the long term they may lead to another period of retrenchment and a wave of plant closures. For example, in early 1988 Philips, Europe's largest consumer electronics company, disclosed its plans to shed 20 000 jobs and close 70 factories worldwide by 1993. In contrast, European subsidiaries of Japanese electronics companies (e.g. Hitachi, JVC, Sanyo and Sony) have already attained productivity levels that are the envy of Western producers. Consequently, numerous European firms are losing their market share and facing a massive excess capacity problem. This trend may be reinforced once Korean foreign direct investment takes off.

As competition intensifies, there may well be an increase in defensive mergers. For example, in autos, France's Peugeot and Renault could merge, and the two major US producers, General Motors and Ford, could merge their European car operations with those of either Volkswagen or Fiat. On the other hand, perhaps a more likely outcome is for Western companies to form and/or consolidate strategic alliances with oriental companies. Whatever the solution, rationalization of European production facilities may be essential.

The third key trend in foreign direct investment since the mid-1980s has been the huge increase in international takeovers involving European buyers (i.e. US acquisitions by Europeans, and cross-border deals in Europe itself). This boom reflects the current corporate obsession with global brands and market dominance.[3] In order to become global market-leaders, the giant corporations of the 1980s are pursuing a strategy of geographical diversification and product consolidation. This strategy leads to horizontal mergers (i.e. buying divisions/firms in related businesses) and to the divestment of peripheral business units. The former is likely to result in functional (e.g. marketing, production, sales) overlaps. In both instances, plant closures may be necessary.

Having reviewed the attractions of foreign direct investment, and its main flows in the 1980s, it is suggested here that current trends will eventually lead to a period of painful retrenchment, not dissimilar to that which ravaged Europe in the late 1970s and early 1980s. Given this gloomy prediction, the other chapters in this book are devoted to illustrating the lessons that MNCs, employees' representatives and policy-makers can learn from previous experiences of foreign divestment. The case study material may also prove illuminating to students of business-orientated disciplines.

1.2 The need for, and purpose of, this book

This book may prove helpful to both multinationals and employee representatives involved in the foreign divestment process. A recent example of a 'foreign divestment' may serve to highlight the opportunities and threats that this situation offers to multinationals and trade unions.

In October 1987, Ford, the world's second largest auto company, announced its plans to locate an electronics plant in Dundee, Scotland, which would create 450 jobs. Competition among European nations, including Portugal and Spain, had been particularly acute for this project. Ford's decision represented a major triumph for Locate in Scotland, the agency responsible for attracting inward investment. Six months later, however, Ford had changed its mind and the Dundee investment was scrapped; in early August 1988, it was revealed that the project would instead go to Spain.[4]

After its original announcement, the Detroit-based company had consistently reiterated that the project was conditional upon the British trade unions accepting the single-union deal which Ford had negotiated with the Amalgamated Engineering Union (AEU). No such approval was forthcoming from the unions, and the company decided not to proceed with the project.

The media in Britain sympathized with the US company, and lambasted the unions for their intransigence. Some observers claimed, however, that the single-union deal had been a convenient smoke-screen, and that in reality Ford itself no longer wished to locate in the UK. Advocates of this 'conspiracy theory' alleged that Ford was skilfully redressing the balance of power after its humiliating defeat, only weeks earlier, at the hands of its British employees: industrial action at all 22 of its UK plants, which had also disrupted production on the Continent, had forced Ford to back down in major negotiations over pay and conditions. Others suggested that a foreign government had made Ford a better offer to win the investment originally intended for Dundee.

Surely, though, had union leaders suspected that Ford had an ulterior motive in abandoning the Dundee investment, they would have sought to expose the truth, rather than continue to provide the company with a good reason to call off the project.

Debate will no doubt continue as to why Ford abandoned the Dundee project; the case reveals the tension that can exist between a MNC and employees' representatives. It also illustrates that multinationals such as Ford can implement sensitive decisions without damage to their reputation. This is unlikely to be achieved, however, without the utmost planning. Like the grand chessmaster, the key to success lies in being able to anticipate every move and to devise game-winning tactics. The case studies in this book show that some firms neglected such planning, and that this failure had disastrous consequences for their reputation in Britain, if not in Europe. Others, in contrast, devised and executed a meticulously prepared divestment strategy. For example, prior to press conferences, all possible questions were identified and ready-made answers prepared for all corporate spokesmen; contingency plans were concluded to cover every eventuality. As the cases show, these companies effected plant closure without damage to their image.

Employees' representatives too may learn from the case studies, by gaining a better understanding of corporate decision-making, and by analysing the performance of their colleagues in previous divestment situations. The latter may help them avoid the repetition of previous errors, and some may suggest that the recent Ford case indicates that this is an urgent requirement. Of course, given the far-ranging effects of foreign direct investment and those involved with and affected by foreign subsidiaries (e.g. communities, customers, policy-makers, suppliers), the book may also benefit those who have an interest in anticipating major corporate decisions.

A unique feature of this study is its contribution to a major policy debate that has raged in all the Triad countries (Europe, Japan and the USA). The cause of this transitional verbal battle, and of the heated exchanges between Europe's labour movement and the world's corporate giants, has been the European Commission's draft directive on Employee Disclosure and Consultation, which was prepared by the Dutch former commissioner, Henk Vredeling. The European Parliament has approved the diluted 1983 version, but in order for it to become legislation, *all* EC member-governments must agree to accept the Vredeling Proposals.

Vredeling's main opponent, the UK government, argues that Vredeling is inappropriate to British industrial relations precisely because it proposes legislation rather than a voluntarist approach. The government has indeed argued that Vredeling is unnecessary precisely because MNCs already adhere to guidelines issued by the International Labour Office (ILO) and the Organization for Economic Co-operation and Development (OECD).

In the past, the European Trade Union Confederation (ETUC) has presented a number of carefully selected plant closures to highlight the alleged inadequacy of national legislation and of the Guidelines.[5] All of these celebrated cases occurred in continental Europe. This study, on the other hand, focuses exclusively on large plant closures in the UK. The causes of each closure are identified, and the employee disclosure and consultation practice of these firms is assessed. It is hoped that the results of this study may prove valuable to those embroiled in the current debate on the efficacy of the Guidelines and the need for and desirability of Vredeling.

1.3   Outline of the book

Chapter 2 considers the theoretical explanation of foreign direct investment. By identifying its causes, it is possible to identify some of the likely causes of foreign divestment. The chapter also includes a review of the empirical work on foreign divestment, and highlights the difficulties involved in implementing a foreign divestment decision.

Chapter 3 focuses on the legal and voluntary measures that MNCs should adhere to when issuing redundancies in the UK. Current UK legislation is considered, but the heart of the chapter is devoted to a critique of the OECD's Guidelines, and the European Commission's Vredeling Proposals.

Chapters 4–7 examine 14 closures, involving 11 MNCs from 5 different home countries, in the following sectors: man-made fibres; domestic appliance and consumer electronics; tyre and rubber products; and agricultural and earth-moving equipment. The case study findings are related to the material presented in Chapters 2 and 3. They detail the conduct of foreign divestors in the UK and allow an assessment of current UK legislation and the OECD's Guidelines for Multinational Enterprises. With this insight of the divestment process, one can identify whether the controversial Vredeling Proposals are desirable and necessary.

The final chapter offers an overall summary, providing recommendations to MNCs, trade unions and policy-makers.

References

1. S. J. Gray and M. C. McDermott, 'International mergers and takeovers: a review of trends and recent developments', *European Management Journal*, Spring 1988, pp. 26–43.
2. M. C. McDermott, *Foreign Divestment and Employee Disclosure and Consultation in the UK, 1979–85*, doctoral thesis, University of Glasgow, 1986.
3. M. C. McDermott and S. J. Gray, 'International brands in international takeovers', *Acquisitions Monthly*, August 1988, pp. 24–5.
4. *Glasgow Herald*, 5 August 1988, p. 1.
5. European Trade Union Confederation, *Apercu et documentation sur des cas des conflits dans les filiates Europeenes de groupes multi-nationaux*, Brussels, 1982.

2
Foreign divestment: the theory and the practice

2.1 Introduction

In 1960, US companies accounted for almost half (i.e. 47 per cent) of the total world stock of foreign direct investment. In 1985 the USA was still the largest home country, with 35 per cent of the total stock of fdi, but its relative decline contrasts with the rise of Japan as an important home for multinational corporations: whereas in 1960 Japan accounted for less than 1 per cent, by 1985 it accounted for almost 12 per cent of the world's total fdi stock.

In the late 1980s, US companies remain a major source of fdi in Europe, but there have been some changes in the sectoral distribution of their fdi. Even traditional investors, such as Ford, are investing in advanced electronics, while the newly founded Compaq (established in 1982 and the world's fastest growing company) chose Scotland as its European manufacturing base.

Investments by Compaq, Digital, Hewlett-Packard, Motorola and other high-tech US companies partly compensate for divestment by those in mature sectors, such as Singer, which ceased all European sewing machine production. This example illustrates, in one way, the 'product life-cycle' (PLC) concept, and its application to foreign divestment. In other words, companies establish a manufacturing presence wherever there is high demand, but conversely, once demand weakens, divestment is likely to occur.

Closures of more than 100 foreign-owned plants in the UK have been examined by this author. In addition to the companies featured in the case studies that follow, other large MNCs (e.g. Black & Decker, Ciba-Geigy, General Motors, Hoechst, ITT, Levi-Strauss, Nabisco, Peugeot and SKF) have closed plants in the UK. Time and time again, a plant 'life-cycle effect' can be identified. New foreign-owned plants tend to achieve their production and employment targets rapidly, but this is followed by periods of slower growth, and eventually by closure. O'Malley's research of the Irish experience confirms this pattern.[1] A similar conclusion was reached by Torneden and Boddewyn, who stressed that managers should not consider their enterprises as eternal.[2] It has been suggested that divestment is likely to occur not when a product has no competitive advantage, but at *any* point of transition in the life-cycle. *Any* major change in demand for a product may precipitate a review of the product's future.

The PLC concept also suggests that the same product will be at various stages of its life in different markets. Accordingly, countries may be expected to attract foreign direct investment in different sectors according to the national level of economic development (e.g. Singer ceased sewing machine manufacture in Europe to locate in the Third World). This is too simplistic, however, and not even accurate. Foreign subsidiaries of MNCs in the less developed countries do not make products only for domestic consumption. Often these countries, particularly in the Far East, serve as a source for sophisticated products in developed countries (e.g. in addition to Scotland, Compaq's other foreign operation is in Singapore).

The implications of the plant 'life-cycle' are grave, especially as some product life-cycles contract. It is most unlikely that any recently established foreign-owned manufacturing facility in any country will be in operation for almost 100 years, as was the case with Singer Clydebank.[3] Indeed, such is the rate of technological change in the high-tech industries that plants are likely to prove viable for much shorter durations.

If everyone accepts the inevitability of foreign-owned plant closures, then all parties can benefit. Management and employees will be psychologically prepared, and the latter can seek to avoid redundancy by moving to plants at a more favourable stage in their life-cycle. For those involved in attracting investment, the message is that new inward investment should perhaps be regarded in the long term as a substitute for, rather than a supplement to, existing foreign-owned manufacturing facilities.

In order to appreciate the causes of foreign *divestment*, an understanding of foreign direct *investment* theory is necessary. Although fdi theory is much more developed than foreign divestment theory, even *it* fails to take full account of the numerous complex influences that can lead companies to locate overseas. This book is not, however, a substitute for an international business textbook, and the theoretical aspect of international business is kept to a minimum.

This chapter also highlights the difficulties that executives face in implementing the foreign divestment process. Of course, announcing a plant closure is unlikely to be popular among those affected—the work-force, the local community, suppliers, the host country's government. The company has to strike a proper balance in notifying its employees; premature disclosure could lead to effective resistance, while secrecy can also provoke an extreme reaction among the work-force. It will be seen in the case studies in Chapters 4–7 that, according to the perception of employees, MNCs provided too little information, too late. On the other hand, there have been cases where employees paid no heed to company statements, and thereby precipitated closure.

2.2   Foreign direct investment theory

Since Hymer wrote his seminal thesis on fdi theory in 1960, there have been many and regular contributions to the theoretical development of the MNC.[4]

Nevertheless, in 1981 Calvet concluded that foreign direct investment occurs as 'the result of several forces that no single theory can encompass'.[5] In the course of the 1980s, no major theoretical insights have emerged,[6] and thus Dunning's 'Eclectic Model of International Production' remains one of the most comprehensive tools for analysing and explaining patterns of fdi.[7]

According to Dunning, firms engage in international production when all three of the following conditions or advantages prevail:

— the firm possesses ownership-specific advantage (O);
— it is more profitable to internalize these advantages within the firm than sell them to independent parties; i.e. the firm possesses internalization advantages (I); and
— there are certain benefits to be gained by exploiting the advantages outside the home country market; i.e. the firm possesses location-specific advantages (L).

Ownership-specific advantages exist when an inward investor possesses advantages that are not shared by indigenous competitors. For example, many US multinational corporations have marketing skills that are often lacking in European companies, while many Japanese MNCs outstrip Europeans in production engineering. The costs involved in trying to pass these skills on to another party are such that it is more profitable for the owners to take full responsibility for overseas production. Some companies, however, lack the resources to exploit their advantage and are forced to license out their ownership advantage (e.g. Pilkington licensed its revolutionary float-glass process, while Rowntree licensed its best-selling brands in the USA to America's Hershey). Finally, circumstances in the domestic and foreign market can encourage firms to locate overseas. For example, faced with rising labour costs at home and anti-dumping duties in the European Community, there are great location-specific advantages in South Korean firms locating in the EC.

To recapitulate, all three of these advantages (O, I and L) must be present for foreign direct investment to occur. The eclectic/OIL model of international production applies not only to investment, but also to foreign divestment.

2.3 Foreign divestment theory

Boddewyn has reversed Dunning's 'eclectic theory' to develop one of foreign divestment.[8] According to his 'reverse theory', foreign divestment takes place whenever one of the following three situations arises:

1. a firm loses net competitive advantages over firms of other nationalities;
2. even if it retains them, it no longer finds it beneficial to use them itself; that is, it no longer considers it profitable to 'internalize' these advantages;
3. it no longer finds it profitable to utilize its internalized net competitive advantage outside its home country; it is now more advantageous to

supply foreign markets by exports and the home market by domestic production, or to abandon foreign and/or home markets altogether.[9]

Boddewyn classifies existing theoretical models of foreign divestment into three types in terms of their emphasis: the *conditions* or prerequisites for divestment; the *motivations* for divestment; and a divestment's immediate *precipitating circumstances*.

Condition-based theory

Wilson identified two types of fdi: *active* investment, to exploit a competitive advantage, and *reactive*, which aims to maintain industry stability.[10] He hypothesized that divestment would occur when the reasons for the original investment had been eroded. Thus, manufacturing plants that were active investments are likely to be divested as market competition increases and competitive advantage is lost. On the other hand, for reactive investments, the probability of divestment grows as the structure of the industry changes. It will be seen in Chapters 4–7 that all of the manufacturing plants examined in the case studies were originally *active* investments.

Changes in the foreign business environment are undoubtedly a key divestment factor. These include, for example, declining demand in the home or host markets (e.g. Renault divested American Motors Corporation because of low sales in the US market); spiralling energy costs (e.g. a wave of divestments in the chemical industry in the 1970s); nationalism and increased government regulation (e.g. IBM pulled out of India); and political instability (e.g. large-scale withdrawal from South Africa in 1986–7).

Changing market conditions therefore often result in the loss of location-specific advantages. One study, based on a random sample of 32 MNCs (21 US firms, 9 European and 2 from elsewhere) known to have divestment experience, noted that divestment was due largely to a combination of adverse environmental conditions and poor performance. Of course, the former bears very heavily on the latter. The other key divestment factors were internal to the firm. For example, many divestments arose from ill-advised acquisitions, or perhaps firms decided to concentrate on their core business and divest peripheral units.[11]

Management, however, tends to exaggerate the importance of external factors. This is understandable, as firms are reluctant to blame divestment on bad management, poor products or other internal factors.

The case studies in Chapters 4–7 suggest that many UK plant closures have been caused by changing demand patterns which resulted in the loss of location-specific advantages and excess capacity for the MNCs involved.

Motivation-based theory

While Boddewyn's work tends to pay particular attention to 'condition-based theory', other authors have emphasized the motivations for foreign divestment.[12] For example, Grunberg stresses that a subsidiary's ability to succeed in the internal environment of intra-corporate rivalry is just as important for its survival as its performance in the external environment.[13] Failure in either market will inevitably lead to sub-standard performance and ultimately to divestment.

Poor subsidiary performance is the most frequently cited reason for foreign divestment; it was mentioned by 94 per cent of the 32 MNCs in the *Business International* study as the key factor triggering divestment.[14] Similarly, Torneden reported that 60 per cent of the US firms he interviewed listed it as the primary causal factor,[15] and Sachdev in his study of UK foreign divestment also stressed poor subsidiary performance.[16]

A decline in parent company earnings or, worse still, the prospect of losses often leads to rationalization throughout the group (e.g. General Motors, IBM, and Philips in the late 1980s), especially of overseas operations. Under such circumstances, some parents adopt a last-in, first-out policy. This usually results in the divestment of a foreign subsidiary.

Corporate strategy has been transformed, however, since the above studies were published, let alone written. Many MNCs have adopted a global strategy which demands that a subsidiary or plant be evaluated not in isolation, but rather as a contributor to the whole entity. Assessment becomes even more problematic when manufacturing is closely integrated, as say with the European operations of Ford.

Poor pre-investment analysis also explains many divestments. The upsurge in the number of US foreign divestments during the 1970s was due to the acquisition binge of the 1960s. Kitching found that at least 25 per cent of a large sample of US acquisitions in Europe were subsequently judged failures for lack of sufficient consideration of external and corporate factors.[17] Similarly, several European companies also appear to have made major blunders in their US acquisitions, which were eventually divested.

Structural and organizational factors also rank as prominent causal factors of foreign divestment. Financial or operating problems in the parent company, or lack of managerial and capital resources to sustain foreign operations, were cited as reasons for divestment by 41 per cent of respondents in the *Business International* study, and poor managerial performance by both local and expatriate managers was mentioned as a reason for foreign divestment by 13 per cent of the respondents in the study.

Precipitating-circumstance-based theory

For many managers, the decision to divest is the most difficult they will ever make.[18] In the past, managers suspected that their superiors and shareholders viewed divestment as an admission of defeat. They believed that divestment bore the stigma of failure.

Pride is not the only emotion to interfere with decision-making. Managerial sentiment is a crucial deterrent (or 'exit barrier') to divestment. It inhibits divestment to such an extent that the removal of certain executives may be essential for divestment to occur. In the Goodyear Drumchapel plant closure, the chairman's past connections with the plant were certainly reflected in the US MNC's divestment strategy. Management's concern with the social and economic consequences of the divestment decision appears to have delayed Akzo and Goodyear from closing their plants in Northern Ireland. Last but not least, management's own interests may be adversely affected by divestment. It is understandable therefore that managers in some situations refrain from divesting even when economic logic suggests they should.

A number of researchers have stressed the importance of the appointment of the 'new man', psychologically detached from any particular operation, who overcomes the 'barriers to exit', and is ready to consider divestment.[19] According to Boddewyn, the rapid inflation of the 1970s resulted in a shift in the balance of power within MNCs to the advantage of the treasurer/financial controller.[20] Consequently, these more cost-conscious executives often effected a change in corporate strategy that involved divestment of poorly performing divisions, or 'dogs', to use the jargon of the day.

Other 'exit barriers' include hard-to-sell assets and integrated units. In the Singer Clydebank closure, the size and age of the plant precluded its sale to another manufacturer, but by isolating the Scottish plant from its other European operations, Singer removed an 'exit barrier'.

Long-established operations which were instrumental in the company's development are particularly likely to secure excessive identification by managers.[21] Wilson found that subsidiaries established by the parent company were less likely to be divested than those acquired from other firms.[22] Acquisitions require comparatively little in the way of managerial resources, and thus 'greenfield' operations are more likely to invoke strong feelings of identification at all levels of the corporate hierarchy. All but 2 of the 14 plant closures examined in this book were originally greenfield investments.

Summary of foreign divestment theory

Foreign divestment theory encapsulates all divestments, not just plant closures. Most relevant research has focused on cases of divestment in the late 1960s and early 1970s, when MNCs had a very limited notion of the potential benefits to be gained from a successful divestment strategy. These studies found that most divestments were *defensive*, though a significant proportion were for strategic reasons.

In recent years *offensive*, or strategic, divestments have become much more common, as firms yet again change their tactics. This is due largely to the changing corporate views on acquisitions. During the 1960s/1970s, the acquisition policy of most MNCs was to achieve geographical consolidation and product diversification. In the late 1980s, the reverse is true: the world's largest corporations are pursuing geographical diversification and product consolidation. Thus, peripheral businesses are divested as companies aim to achieve dominance in their chosen sector(s).[23]

The largest foreign-owned plant closures in the UK seem to have been defensive in nature, in the sense that closure was seen as a means of resolving a problem. In virtually all cases, market conditions had changed substantially since the original investments were made. At the same time, losses at one or more levels in the MNC (parent, subsidiary or plant) provided strong incentives to rationalize UK operations. The UK plant closures often followed shortly after the appointment of a new chief executive at the parent company. In other words, rather than acting as preventive medicine, the closures were tantamount to corporate strategy.

2.4 Foreign divestment in practice

This section examines the foreign divestment decision-making process, and the subsequent implementation of that decision. It highlights the normal pattern of disclosure, first within the corporate hierarchy and then to employees in the host country. Factors determining the timing of disclosure are also considered, for multinationals divesting in foreign countries are walking a tightrope: while they are eager to avoid premature disclosure which may upset their plans, they have a vested interest in being seen as acting with social responsibility. Of course, in reality there is no perfect time for announcing a plant closure; there will always be a hostile reaction from some source. However, a well-planned divestment strategy can succeed in deflecting attention away from the company, and on to another body or individual(s).

The foreign divestment process

A foreign divestment review is usually conducted at the behest of the parent company and unknown to the foreign subsidiary. Parent company executives sometimes seek to postpone informing managers of the subsidiary affected by the divestment decision, especially if they are nationals of the host country.

The length of the foreign divestment process can be defined as the amount of time between the president's or chief executive officer's first consideration of a possible divestment and the moment when the divestment is substantially completed. Torneden found that, on average, the first stage of the foreign divestment process—deciding which plant(s), if any, to divest—took 15 months, while the second stage—implementing the decision—took 10.5 months.[24] Of the 32 MNCs reviewed in the *Business International* study, 15 estimated the first stage as taking 11 months,[25] while, on average, the second stage took 9 months. Most respondents stressed that results worsened and prospects of improvement receded during the two to four years preceding formal divestment analysis. Nees, in an investigation of 14 specific divestment cases, found that the divestment process ranged most frequently from 20 months to several years.[26]

The length of the divestment decision-making process is likely to be shorter if companies have previous divestment experience and/or information systems that allow speedy detection of problems, and/or possible divestment opportunities.[27]

Time spent in deciding is commensurate with the potential and size of the plant/subsidiary. Therefore the divestment process of a unit serving a regional market, such as Europe, the Far East or North America, would tend to be given greater consideration than one serving a national market in, say, Italy, Japan or Canada.

The product range also determines the extent of the divestment process, since greater stigma is attached to management that has to acknowledge failure in its own field of expertise. Conversely, the divestment process is carried out with greater alacrity in a peripheral business, where failure is more readily accepted owing to management's comparatively limited experience.

Foreign divestment and employee disclosure

By giving advance notice to workers facing redundancy, employers can confer significant benefits on those affected. Workers are offered time to brace themselves financially and psychologically for the readjustment that closure demands. Also, while still in employment, their job-hunting efforts are likely to prove more fruitful than those of people who are already unemployed; research confirms that companies prefer to recruit people already in employment. They can also obtain references and counselling from their employer during the advance notice period.[28]

On the other hand, advance notice has its drawbacks for the firm. It may shake the confidence of financial institutions and customers, precipitating a spiral decline in production. It may also have an adverse effect on employees' motivation—but it can have precisely the opposite effect! One executive attributed closure partly to the indolence of the labour force and very poor labour relations, but said that as soon as news of the divestment decision was disclosed the plant became a hive of activity, and labour could not have been more co-operative.

In cases of centralized decision-making, once the decision to close an overseas plant has been reached, the chief executive of the parent company has various options to choose from. He can keep his decision secret and let foreign subsidiary management believe that no such decision has been taken, or he can reveal the news to whatever levels in the corporate hierarchy he considers it expedient to inform, with the specific instruction that it remain confidential. Then again, he may inform subsidiary management and empower them to break the news to employees whenever appropriate; or he may directly inform those affected by his decision.

This example presumes centralized decision-making, but some firms have a decentralized decision-making structure which permits subsidiary management to allocate resources or withhold them. A major problem facing trade union representatives is verifying whether major decisions have been made at parent company level or by subsidiary management. This uncertainty may breed suspicion.

Employee disclosure and consultation is deeply complex, especially in the foreign-owned plant closure situation. Trade union officials may be suspicious of corporate information received from sources other than the chief executive of the parent company.

Employees and their representatives are interested, first and foremost, in information relating to the terms, conditions, scale, security and location of employment.[29] Consumption and life-style are determined by present and anticipated income, so employees are particularly anxious when uncertainty surrounds the future of their place of work. In order to avoid unexpected redundancies, trade unions want meaningful information on the performance of individual plants, which will allow them to evaluate the likelihood of job losses and total closure. When closure or redundancies are very unexpected, employees may resort to unlawful action; for example, employees at Caterpillar, Glasgow, staged a sit-in.

One particular case of extreme employee reaction to proposed redundancies—though a domestic divestment—involved Peugeot at its Poissy factory, near Paris. In late 1983, France's second largest car manufacturer announced that redundancies would be forthcoming at its Talbot plant. The reaction of the multi-racial work-force was extreme, heightening racial tension in the country and allowing more extreme political parties to gain momentum. Violent clashes broke out between immigrants (who formed 80 per cent of the work-force, and whose strike action was backed by the pro-Socialist CFDT union) and the white, indigenous workers (who were backed by the Communist-led CGT union). The conflict was extensively covered by television, which showed rival factions armed with guns and slings being separated by riot police, who had to resort to the use of CS gas.

Eighteen months later, at least 100 people were injured, some seriously, when clashes broke out between riot police and militant members of the pro-Communist CGT union at SKF's Ivry factory on the outskirts of Paris. The Swedish MNC's ball-bearing plant had been occupied throughout the previous 18 months by the CGT and the Communists in a bid to avert its closure.

The Talbot and SKF cases clearly highlight the potential problems of plant closures involving major job losses.

2.5 Summary

From this review of the foreign divestment process, a number of conclusions can be drawn. First, a divestment review is usually conducted at the behest of the parent company and unknown to the foreign subsidiary. Second, parent company executives sometimes seek to postpone informing managers of the subsidiary affected by the divestment decision, especially if they are natives of the host country. Third, establishing the length of the divestment process is difficult because executives were unable to pin-point the start of the process, but one investigation of 14 specific divestment cases found that the process ranged most frequently from 20 months to several years. Another investigation found that, on average, 20.5 months is the length of the divestment process for US multinational corporations.

The fact that the divestment decision is centralized and enshrouded in secrecy sometimes results in the parent company withholding details of decisions from subsidiary management for as long as they consider expedient. This time lag is repeated down the line until the decision reaches employees. MNCs withdrawing completely from a host country are likely to disregard employee disclosure and consultation.

It is worth noting here that previous research found that US and European MNCs have different ideas of what constitutes good behaviour. US multinationals believe that the mere fulfilling of legal obligations satisfies the requirements of good corporate citizenship. European MNCs, on the other hand, were said to have a more pronounced sense of social responsibility. Although the theme is not developed in this work, preliminary findings do suggest that the national culture of the home country is sometimes reflected in the corporation's divestment strategy.

References

1. 'Shamrock lure attracts foreign companies', *Financial Times*, 18 March 1986.
2. R. L. Torneden and J. J. Boddewyn, 'US foreign disinvestment: a preliminary survey', *Columbia Journal of World Business*, 25–29, Summer 1973.
3. M. C. McDermott, *Singer's Clydebank: Anatomy of Closure*, Undergraduate dissertation, University of Glasgow, 1982.
4. S. H. Hymer, *A Study of Direct Foreign Investment*, MIT Press, Cambridge, Mass, 1976.
5. A. L. Calvet, 'A synthesis of FDI theories and theories of the multinational firm', *Journal of International Business Studies*, 43–58, Spring–Summer 1981.
6. M. Casson, *The Firm and the Market*, Blackwell, Oxford, 1987; S. Young, Private papers reviewing major issues and trends in foreign direct investment, 1988.
7. J. H. Dunning, *International Production and the Multinational Enterprise*, Allen & Unwin, London, 1981.
8. J. J. Boddewyn, 'Notes on a theory of foreign divestment', annual meeting of Academy of Management, Dallas, August 1983.
9. Ibid., p. 3.
10. B. D. Wilson, *Disinvestment of Foreign Subsidiaries*, UMI Research Press, Ann Arbor, 1980.

11. Business International, *International Divestment: A Survey of Corporate Experience*, 1976, p. 12.
12. L. Grunberg, *Failed Multinational Ventures: The Political Economy of International Divestments*, Lexington Books, D. C. Heath, Lexington, 1981; N. Hood and S. Young, *Multinationals in Retreat: The Scottish Experience*, Edinburgh University Press, 1982.
13. L. Grunberg, op. cit.
14. Business International, op. cit.
15. R. L. Torneden, *Foreign Disinvestment by US Multinational Corporations*, Praeger, New York, 1975.
16. J. C. Sachdev, *A Framework for the Planning of Disinvestment Policies of Multinational Companies*, doctoral thesis, UMIST, 1976.
17. J. Kitching, *Acquisitions in Europe: Causes of Corporate Successes and Failures*, Business International, Geneva, 1983.
18. J. L. Bower, *Managing the Resource Allocation Process*, Harvard University Graduate School of Business Administration, Division of Research Publication, Boston, 1970; S. C. Gilmour, *The Divestment Decision Process*, DBA Dissertation, Harvard University Graduate School of Business Administration, 1973; R. L. Torneden, op. cit., B. D. Wilson, op. cit.
19. J. J. Boddewyn, 'Divestment: local vs. foreign and US vs. European Approaches', *Management International Review*, 1, 21–27, 1979; and, Foreign Divestment: Magnitude Factors', *Journal of International Business Studies*, 10, 1, Spring–Summer 1979; S. C. Gilmour, op. cit.; R. H. Hilman and J. V. Soden, 'Don't try to sell a pig in a poke', *Corporate Financing*, November–December 1971; L. Vignola, *Strategic Divestment*, American Management Association, New York, 1974; H. W. Wallender, 'A planned approach to divestment', *Columbia Journal of World Business*, 33–37, Spring 1973.
20. J. J. Boddewyn, *Journal of International Business Studies*, 1979, op. cit.
21. M. E. Porter, 'Please note the location of nearest exit: exit barriers and planning', *California Management Review*, 21–33, Winter 1976.
22. B. D. Wilson, op. cit.
23. M. C. McDermott and S. J. Gray, 'International takeovers: the pursuit of global market leadership', European Association for Research in Industrial Economics, Erasmus University, Rotterdam, September 1986.
24. R. L. Torneden, op. cit.
25. Business International, op. cit.
26. D. Nees, 'The divestment decision process in large and medium-sized diversified companies: a descriptive model based on clinical studies', *International Studies of Management and Organisation*, 8, 67–95, 1978.
27. Business International, op. cit.
28. A. B. Carrol, 'Managing public affairs when business closes down: social responsibilities and management actions', *California Management Review*, Winter 1984.
29. S. J. Gray, *Information Disclosure and the Multinational Corporation*, Wiley, 1984.

3
The regulatory environment and the OECD's guidelines for multinational enterprises

3.1 Introduction

This chapter outlines employee disclosure and consultation legislation in plant closures resulting in mass dismissals in the UK. It helps to assess the extent to which divesting foreign multinational corporations have adhered to the employee disclosure and consultation requirements contained in Part IV of the 1975 Employment Protection Act (EPA).

The year following the passing of the EPA, the Organization for Economic Co-operation and Development introduced its Guidelines for Multinational Enterprises (hereafter referred to as either 'the OECD's Guidelines' or simply 'the Guidelines'). The critical 'Employment and industrial relations' section of the Guidelines is also evaluated in this chapter.

Another feature of this book is its consideration of the acrimony between Europe's labour movement and the world's corporate giants over the European Commission's 1980 draft directive, 'Proposal for a council directive on procedure for informing and consulting employees of undertakings with complex structures, and in particular transnational undertakings'. This draft directive was prepared by the EC commissioner then responsible for Labour and Social Affairs, Henk Vredeling, and is commonly known as the Vredeling Proposals.

3.2 UK employee disclosure and consultation legislation in the plant closure context

The 1975 Employment Protection Act consists of five parts and 129 sections. Part IV, 'Procedure for handling redundancies', is the critical section in regard to the issues raised here.

The duty to consult with trade union representatives arises when an employer proposes to dismiss as redundant 'an employee of a description in respect of which an independent trade union is recognised by him' (Section 99 (1)).

Consultations with trade union representatives should begin at 'the earliest opportunity'. In cases where the employer is proposing to dismiss as redundant 100 or more employees at one establishment within a period of 90 days or less, consultation should begin at least 90 days before the first of those dismissals takes effect. This timetable is for dismissals within one 'establishment', but no definition is offered of this imprecise concept.

Although employers are bound to begin consultations 'at the earliest possible opportunity', no guidance is offered on what constitutes 'the earliest opportunity'. The Department of Employment overlooks this stipulation, and is quite satisfied as long as firms provide the minimum notice.

The employer must disclose the following information to trade union representatives for the purpose of consultation: (1) the reasons for his proposals; (2) the numbers and descriptions of employees whom it is proposed to dismiss as redundant; (3) the total number of employees of any such description employed by the employer at the establishment in question; (4) the proposed method of selecting the employees who may be dismissed, and (5) the proposed method of carrying out the dismissals, with due regard to any agreed procedure, including the period over which the dismissals are to take effect.

The employer is then required to consider any representation made by trade unions, to reply to those representations, and, if he rejects any, to state his reasons.

3.3 Controlling the multinationals: a 1970s perspective

In the early 1970s, many developing countries discovered that recently gained political independence did not automatically produce economic independence. The pace of economic growth and development was still determined largely by decisions made in boardrooms of distant continents. This predicament is almost glorified in an advertising campaign for the tropical fruit company of RJR-Nabisco, the US tobacco-to-foods giant, which depicts a figure dressed in radiant white, 'the man from Del Monte', descending from the skies to consent to the gathering of the crop. LDCs wanted to break the umbilical cord of economic dependence, and they campaigned for greater controls on MNCs.

Given that most multinationals have their headquarters in an OECD member-country, the decision in 1976 by the OECD to issue guidelines for MNCs may at first seem at odds with the interests of OECD members. But the speed at which they were formulated was in anticipation of more rigorous controls which the UN might impose; the motives of OECD were therefore suspect right from the start.[1]

The OECD initiative cannot however be explained simply by external pressure: there was growing concern about the activities of MNCs even within OECD countries. The reputation of US multinational corporations had been severely tarnished by the Lockheed bribery scandal involving senior members of the Japanese government, and by ITT's involvement in the Chilean coup of 1973.

Furthermore, some leading politicians in OECD countries called for a code of conduct for MNCs, or were very critical of certain multinationals based in their own country. In September 1973 Helmut Schmidt, then Germany's minister of finance, argued that such a measure was necessary to ensure that multinationals did not 'shirk their obligations to the countries of residence'. Two years later, the then US secretary of state, Henry Kissinger, proposed a code as one of the main themes of his addresses to the General Assembly of the United Nations.[2] The activity in Africa of Lonrho, a British MNC, was denounced by the then Conservative prime minister of Britain, Edward Heath, as the 'unacceptable face of capitalism'.

Appeals for greater governmental control of international business grew and began to find popular support within OECD countries. Indeed, labour unions were becoming increasingly anxious about the 'export of jobs' and the lack of access to the real decision-makers. They contended that this situation rendered national employee disclosure and consultation legislation meaningless. This problem was particularly acute in cases of projected plant closure.

Some OECD countries (i.e. Canada, the Netherlands and the Scandinavian countries) thus favoured legal controls over MNCs. These countries did not share the ulterior motives of a rival faction, led by the USA with Britain, Japan, Switzerland and West Germany in tow, which resisted regulation. Securing voluntary status for the Guidelines represented a significant victory for the latter camp.[3] It is worth bearing this division in mind when one comes to the case studies.

3.4   The OECD's Guidelines for Multinational Enterprises

The OECD, founded in 1961, comprises member-countries from the rich, industrialized 'North'; poor, developing countries from the 'South' are conspicuously absent (see Table 3.1). During the early 1970s there were groups in both 'North' and 'South' calling for restrictions on multinational corporations.

Table 3.1   Members of the OECD

Australia	France	Japan	Spain
Austria	West Germany	Luxembourg	Sweden
Belgium	Greece	The Netherlands	Switzerland
Canada	Iceland	New Zealand	Turkey
Denmark	Ireland	Norway	United Kingdom
Finland	Italy	Portugal	USA

The scope, status and administration of the Guidelines

The Guidelines suggested a code of procedure in dealing with: the disclosure of information; competition; financing; taxation; employment and industrial relations; and science and technology. They were part of the 'Declaration and decisions on international investment and multinational enterprises', a package designed to foster an environment favourable to foreign direct investment and MNCs. 'Declarations' are not included among the legal instruments of the OECD, but 'Decisions' of the OECD Council are 'legally binding on the member states of the Organization by virtue of its constituent treaty'. The package included 'Decisions' on 'National treatment', 'International investment incentives and disincentives' and 'International consultation procedures'. The Guidelines themselves, however, form an appendix to the 'Declaration' and as such are not legally binding. Indeed, the introduction states that 'Observance of the Guidelines is voluntary and not legally enforceable.'[4]

The Committee on International Investment and Multinational Enterprises (CIME), administers these Guidelines. Its prime function is confined to clarifying, on request, sections of the Guidelines. It was denied any judicial function, and was expressly forbidden from commenting on the conduct of an individual enterprise.[5] These limitations on the Guidelines' watchdog did little to inspire confidence in the OECD's initiative.

Administration and promotion of the Guidelines has been somewhat decentralized since 1979 when a 'National contact point' (NCP) was established in each OECD country. Each NCP is responsible for promoting and explaining the Guidelines to the business community and labour organizations of its country.

The Trades Union Advisory Committee (TUAC), which represents labour's interests at the OECD, has been very critical of the NCPs in most OECD countries. It singled out five countries in which the unions had been actively assisted and consulted by the NCP: Belgium, Denmark, Finland, the Netherlands and Sweden. With the exception of Belgium, these were the very countries that had supported OECD legislation, rather than mere Guidelines, for MNCs. Significantly, according to a senior UK executive of the Dutch MNC Akzo (featured in the next chapter), the company stresses the importance of the Guidelines upon its management.

The British Trades Union Congress (TUC) has dismissed the UK National Contact Point as little more than a postbox between unions and management. This is precisely the role it served when the TUC formally complained about Caterpillar's conduct in announcing the closure of its Newcastle plant in 1983 (see Chapter 7).

The author interviewed managers, past and present, of many of the companies featured in Chapters 4–7. Trade union officials involved in the plant closures described in these chapters were also interviewed. With a few exceptions, both management and union officials were, at worst, unaware of the OECD's Guidelines or, at best, unfamiliar with their content. The author's findings suggest that in Britain only the most senior union officials were familiar with the Guidelines. A regional union official involved in the Caterpillar Newcastle closure believed that the Guidelines emanated from the EC. When asked why the British TUC had apparently made so little use of them, he explained that unions could not support them because this might be interpreted as condoning membership of the EC, when the Labour Party was committed to withdrawal from the Community. Following the Caterpillar referral to the UK National Contact Point, the same official concluded that the Guidelines were 'useless', although 'in terms of propaganda they are great'. It is somewhat surprising that British trade unions have not succeeded in educating their officials about the Guidelines.

The 'Employment and industrial relations' section

While the LDCs could directly influence the United Nations, their exclusion from the OECD denied them a say in the drafting of its Guidelines. On the other hand, some OECD countries shared the LDCs' desire that there should be international regulation to control multinationals. Although their appeals for legislation were rejected by the USA and its supporters, the crucial 'Employment and industrial relations' chapter was introduced only to placate 'progressive' OECD member-states, and even then it was liberally scattered with ambiguity, clearly denoting an absence of precept.

Clarification of the 'Employment and industrial relations' section is however unnecessary, regardless of the ambiguity of individual paragraphs, because this section of the Guidelines is qualified by the 'chapeau clause'. The clause commends MNCs to adhere to this section of the Guidelines, but to do so *within the framework of law, regulations and prevailing labour relations and employment practices, in each of the countries in which they operate'.*[6] It is significant that the 'chapeau clause' prefaces only the section of the Guidelines that bears most heavily on protecting the interests of employees.

The 'Employment and industrial relations' section has proved the most controversial part of the Guidelines. (It is reproduced in the Appendix at the end of this chapter.) Paragraph 6 in particular has been one of the most often invoked. TUAC has accused a number of MNCs (e.g. Firestone; Ford), when closing a plant, of failing to provide 'reasonable notice'. In 1979 CIME stated that notice should be given 'prior to the final decision being taken'.[7] It added that, in order to adhere to paragraph 6, enterprises should inform employees of their intention to close plants before their decision is final and irreversible. Paragraph 9 intends that MNCs should either delegate local management with the authority to conduct negotiations or send duly authorized representatives from headquarters for negotiations with the employees.

Despite CIME's 'clarifications', the upshot of the 'chapeau clause' has been that the TUAC has had to challenge the principle that, 'if national legislation exists on items covered by the Guidelines, and if the enterprise has not violated this legislation, then it has automatically respected the Guidelines'.[8] None the less, trade unionists insist on judging firms' conduct against each paragraph of the 'Employment and industrial relations' guidelines, and in so doing have failed to grasp the fundamental impact of the 'chapeau clause' and its neutralizing effect. They have thus failed to appreciate that the 'Employment and industrial relations' section does not override national laws, and therefore fails to provide new rights or obligations to either employees or enterprises. Companies that comply with appropriate national legislation have automatically respected this section of the Guidelines. This is precisely why the umbrella organization for national employers' confederations in the EC, UNICE (L'Union des Industries de la Communaute Europeene), fully supports the Guidelines.

Some members of CIME may genuinely wish the Guidelines to be regarded as supplementary, but the fact is that, until the 'chapeau clause' is removed, they will remain only complementary to national legislation. The 'Employment and industrial relations' guidelines do nothing to inhibit those MNCs that regard minimum legal requirements as a ceiling; for those that aim to respect not just the letter, but the spirit, of the law they are irrelevant. This was precisely the thinking underlying the European Commission's controversial Vredeling Proposals. The author would, however, dispute the contention of Robinson that, 'without the OECD's Guidelines, and in particular the industrial relations section, it is more than likely that the Vredeling move would never have seen the light of day'.[9] Quite the reverse: not only would Vredeling have been published earlier, but its journey through the EC's legislative process would have been smoother, and quicker. For because of the Guidelines, European trade unions and some politicians ignored their instincts and dithered for four years awaiting proof that the Guidelines would solve the inherent contradiction in seeking protection from national legislation in tackling problems with international dimensions.

Campbell and Rowan have concluded that the relatively small number of alleged infractions of the Guidelines 'provides testimony to the generally good comportment, and thus good reputation, of multinational firms'.[10] For the reasons indicated in this chapter, a more mundane conclusion seems appropriate: namely, that MNCs respect national legislation.

Throughout the Vredeling Proposals debate, employers' organizations have argued that further legislation is unnecessary. Often they present the Guidelines and Vredeling as alternatives which differ only in legal status, while being fully aware that, legalities apart, Vredeling threatens to impose much more onerous obligations on companies. Labour organizations have fallen for this ploy. Consequently, they have devoted time and resources haggling over the extent of compliance to the Guidelines, especially the 'Employment and industrial relations' section. This is a futile exercise, for the nine paragraphs of this section are not independent: they are prefaced by the 'chapeau clause', the effect of which is that these Guidelines only *commend* adherence to national legislation. The OECD Guidelines are therefore an irrelevance in the Vredeling debate. The key criterion in establishing the need for Vredeling should be, first, the effectiveness of national legislation, and second, the precision and validity of the draft directive's proposals.

Focus now transfers from the Paris-based OECD to the Brussels-based European Community.

3.5 The European Commission's Vredeling Proposals

By the late 1970s, Henk Vredeling and his allies were arguing the the OECD's Guidelines and the ILO's Tripartite Declaration of Principles had failed to appease labour precisely because of their voluntary nature. He therefore believed that only the EC, with its legislative powers, could redress the balance in favour of employees.

The European Commission recognized that, while employees' information and consultation rights were determined by *national* legislation, the *internationalization* of business and the tendency towards centralized decision-making had rendered national legislation ineffective for many employees.

The Vredeling Proposals called for the regular provision of information— half-yearly at least—covering the following subjects: structure and manning; the economic and financial situation; current and likely development of the business, production, sales and employment; production, investment and restructuring plans; current and proposed manufacturing and working methods; and, finally, all procedures and plans liable to have 'a substantial effect' on employees' interests. Employees would have to be consulted when a proposed decision was liable to have 'a substantial effect' on their interests, e.g. the closure of a plant.

The European Trade Union Confederation has spearheaded labour's campaign to have Vredeling pass through the EC's labyrinth of legal channels and become legislation. Although Vredeling was doomed to a lengthy passage by the EC's cumbersome decision-making process, this was not fully appreciated by American and Japanese business interests. The original proposals had no sooner been submitted than employers' organizations from the USA and Japan lent their full support to the anti-Vredeling group, led by Europe's employers' organizations. The most expensive lobbying campaign ever witnessed by the EC was launched in a frantic bid to bury the draft directive. Large individual MNCs played a prominent role in the campaign, and representatives of US and Japanese companies warned of a reduction in foreign direct investment in the EC, and indeed divestment, if Vredeling was enacted. For example, the Keidanren, the Japanese employers' federation, suggested that 'The directive, if put into effect, could have a restrictive effect on the growth of Japanese investment in Europe.'[11] Concern that Vredeling would discourage fdi in the EC has been echoed by the UK government.[12]

Given the scale of opposition, it came as no surprise when, in the autumn of 1982, the original Vredeling Proposals were somewhat diluted by a number of amendments approved by the European Parliament. This was reflected in the revised version of Vredeling, published the following June under Henk Vredeling's successor, Ivor Richard, the British commissioner.

In late 1983, the revised draft directive was passed by the Commission and the European Parliament. It had therefore reached the final hurdle, but in order to become Community law it must secure *unanimous* approval by the Council of Ministers composed of representatives from all EC governments. Britain's Conservative government remains the main stumbling block to the directive's progress. Moreover, its opposition is based on the Commission's failure to provide evidence that the OECD's Guidelines are 'not working satisfactorily'.

Article 4 of the revised text assumes that all major corporate decisions are centralized. In the plant closure situation, companies would have to go through the following procedure.

Stage 1 The management of the parent would be required to 'forward precise information to the management of the subsidiary concerned in good time before the final decision is taken with a view to the communication of this information to the employees' representatives in the manner provided in paragraph 3 (i.e. communicate in writing)'.[13] Employees' representatives would therefore receive information concerning the proposed decision; the legal, economic and social consequences of such decision for the employees concerned; and the measures planned in respect of such employees.

Stage 2 The management of the subsidiary concerned is then required to communicate in writing, without delay, the information listed above to employees' representatives.

Stage 3 In its written communication, subsidiary management is to ask employees' representatives for their opinion of the proposed decision, giving them a period of at least 30 days from the day on which the information is communicated.

Stage 4 The management of the subsidiary concerned is to hold consultations with employees' representatives with a view to attempting to reach agreement on the measures planned in respect of the employees.

Stage 5 The plant closure decision can only be implemented once the opinion of the employees' representatives has been received, or, failing that, once the minimum 30-day period allowed for in stage 3 has expired.

As with the OECD's Guidelines, key terms in the Vredeling Proposals are imprecise. For example, in Article 4 alone, a number of terms (e.g. 'final decision', 'without delay') are imprecise. Legislation that is riddled with ambiguities, like the revised text, is likely to engender rather than solve problems—a view shared in Britain by both the TUC and the employers' organization, the Confederation of British Industry.

3.6   Summary

This chapter has examined current employee disclosure and consultation requirements for employers in the UK proposing mass dismissals, legislation that is clearly applicable in the plant closure situation. It was seen that the Department of Employment is satisfied so long as companies meet the minimum legal requirements, and makes little effort to ensure that companies abide by the spirit of the law.

The OECD introduced its Guidelines for two reasons. It wanted to dissuade the UN that legal controls on MNCs were necessary, and it had to appease some of its own members who believed that multinationals should be subject to international legislation. The Guidelines have succeeded in that neither the UN nor the EC has adopted the tough legislation that once looked likely. This achievement is all the more remarkable given the limitations imposed on the administrators of the Guidelines, and the diluting effect of the 'chapeau clause'.

The European Commission's Vredeling Proposals were originally intended as a means to compensate for the inadequacies of national legislation and voluntary codes of conduct in the age of international business. Despite the elimination of its more controversial aspects, Vredeling is unlikely to become Community legislation before the mid-1990s, if ever. Since it was first proposed, the EC, in common with many countries throughout the world, has adopted a more conciliatory stance towards MNCs. Environmental protection and merger controls are the areas in which greater EC regulation is likely. The Commission itself seems to have accepted that persevering with Vredeling is futile.

In the past, the Trades Union Advisory Committee at the OECD has presented a number of carefully selected plant closures to highlight the alleged inadequacy of national legislation and of the Guidelines. All of these celebrated cases occurred in continental Europe, but this study focuses on 14 large foreign-owned plant closures in the UK. It is hoped that the results of this study may prove of interest to those embroiled in the current debate on the efficacy of the Guidelines and the need for, and desirability of, Vredeling.

Appendix

The OECD's Guidelines for Multinational Enterprises: the 'Employment and Industrial Relations' section[14]

Enterprises should, within the framework of law, regulations and prevailing labour relations and employment practices, in each of the countries in which they operate,

1. respect the right of their employees to be represented by trade unions and other bona fide organisations of employees, and engage in constructive negotiations, either individually or through employers' associations, with

such employee organisations with a view to reaching agreements on employment conditions, which should include provisions for dealing with disputes arising over the interpretation of such agreements, and for ensuring mutually respected rights and responsibilities;

2. (a) provide such facilities to representatives of the employees as may be necessary to assist in the development of effective collective agreements,
   (b) provide to representatives of employees information which is needed for meaningful negotiations on conditions of employment;

3. provide to representatives of employees, where this accords with local law and practice, information which enables them to obtain a true and fair view of the performance of the entity or, where appropriate, the enterprise as a whole;

4. observe standards of employment and industrial relations not less favourable than those observed by comparable employers in the host country;

5. in their operations, to the greatest extent practicable, utilise, train and prepare for upgrading members of the local labour force in co-operation with representatives of their employees and, where appropriate, the relevant governmental authorities;

6. in considering changes in their operations which would have major effects upon the livelihood of their employees, in particular in the case of the closure of an entity involving collective lay-offs or dismissals, provide reasonable notice of such changes to representatives of their employees, and where appropriate to the relevant governmental authorities, and co-operate with the employee representatives and appropriate governmental authorities so as to mitigate to the maximum extent practicable adverse effects;

7. implement their employment policies including hiring, discharge, pay, promotion and training without discrimination unless selectivity in respect of employee characteristics is in furtherance of established governmental policies which specifically promote greater equality of employment opportunity;

8. in the context of bona fide negotiations with representative of employees on condition of employment, or while employees are exercising a right to organise, not threaten to utilise a capacity to transfer the whole or part of an operating unit from the country concerned nor transfer employees from the enterprise's component entities in other countries in order to influence unfairly those negotiations or to hinder the exercise of a right to organise.

References

1. J. Robinson, *Multinationals and Political Control*, Gower, Aldershot, 1983.
2. S. Dell, 'The state of play on the code of conduct', *Multinationals and European Integration: Speakers Papers*. Conference sponsored by the *Financial Times* IRM, London, 5–6 April 1984.
3. G. Hamilton, 'The control of multinationals: what future for international codes of conduct in the 1980s?', *Multinational Info*, October–December 1984, p. 6.
4. OECD, *International Investment and Multinational Enterprises: Guidelines for Multinational Enterprises*, Paris, 1976, p. 12.

5. OECD, *International Investment and Multinational Enterprises: Review of the 1976 Declaration and Decisions*, Paris, 1979.
6. OECD, 1976, op. cit.; italics mine.
7. OECD, 1979, op. cit., p. 37.
8. TUAC, quoted in D. C. Campbell and R. L. Rowan, *Multinational Enterprises and the OECD Industrial Relations Guidelines*, University of Pennsylvania Press, Philadelphia, 1983, p. 146.
9. Robinson, op. cit., p. 112.
10. Campbell and Rowan, op. cit., p. 12.
11. Institute of Directors Policy Unit, *The Vredeling Proposals and Vth Directive: Comments on the Consultative Document Issues by the Department of Trade and Industry and the Department of Employment*, London, 1984.
12. T. King, Department of Employment, and Trade and Industry press release, 9 November 1983.
13. Commission of the European Communities, *Proposal for a Directive on Procedures for Informing and Consulting the Employees of Undertakings with Complex Structures, in Particular TNCs*, Com (80), 423 Final, Brussels, 23 October 1980.
14. OECD, 1979.

4
The man-made fibre industry

4.1 Introduction

During the 1960s the man-made fibre industry enjoyed boom conditions, with nylon proving to be a particularly popular material. Between 1963 and 1973, synthetics increased from about 40 per cent to 70 per cent of total textile mill output. Producers responded to the market and launched a huge construction programme. This greatly increased the UK industry's capacity, and UK output rose significantly, from 550 000 tonnes in 1969 to a peak of 750 000 tonnes in 1974.

This success was totally overshadowed by the effects of the dramatic price increase in the industry's basic raw material, oil. In the course of 1974, oil prices quadrupled. This sent shock waves throughout the industrialized economies of the world which were, in the main, net importers of 'black gold'. The ramifications of this price increase cannot be overestimated in regard to its effect on the production of nylon.

Problems in the industry as a whole were exacerbated by increased capacity as new plants, born of the 1960s boom conditions, came on stream. By 1978 UK production of man-made fibres was a third down on the level reached in 1974, and in 1979 the synthetic fibre industry in Europe was operating at only 70 per cent capacity. Nylon suffered disproportionately, and the following statistics illustrate the scale of the slump.

Whereas nylon had a 43 per cent share of total synthetic production in 1965, by 1978 it accounted for only 24 per cent. Between 1968 and 1973,

Table 4.1 Performance data on Monsanto PLC, 1974–80 (£'000)

Year	Sales	Pre-tax profit	Post-tax profit
1980	232 901	(29 344)	(29 547)
1979	255 982	(4 196)	(3 942)
1978	211 743	2 610	2 866
1977	202 727	5 562	2 246
1976	180 810	13 992	6 588
1975	122 829	5 713	2 827
1974	121 291	17 192	8 183

Source: Extel Statistical Services

production of nylon filament textiles had grown by 3.7 per cent and nylon filament carpet by 28 per cent; but between 1973 and 1978, the former actually fell by 5.3 per cent, and the latter's rate of growth shrank to a mere 1.3 per cent.

The following case studies examine the consequences of the slump in man-made fibres on the UK plants of Akzo, Holland's third largest company, and Monsanto, America's fourth largest chemical company. The analysis begins by examining Monsanto's handling of the divestment process at its nylon plant at Dundonald, Ayrshire, which opened in 1966 just one year after Monsanto had entered the nylon fibre business.

4.2 Monsanto

Dundonald

Background

In the UK, Monsanto had relatively modest nylon fibre plants and a small market share. Its Dundonald plant had the smallest capacity of any nylon fibre facility in the UK, and Monsanto had only 9 per cent of the UK market, and 4 per cent of the Western European market. The UK nylon fibre market was dominated by two British companies: ICI (48 per cent) and Courtaulds (25 per cent), followed by Akzo's subsidiary, Enka (18 per cent).

Monsanto had responded quickly to the slump that followed the dramatic increase in oil prices. As early as 1974, the work-force at Dundonald was reduced as part of a cost-cutting exercise, and the UK subsidiary remained profitable until the late 1970s. In 1980 Monsanto's UK subsidiary suffered a loss of almost £30 million (see Table 4.1). Indeed, Monsanto's entire European nylon operations had become a loss-making business, and the US parent company was clearly concerned. In its 1978 *Annual Report*, the parent company chairman explained that programmes were being launched to rectify the 'unacceptable losses' of the European nylon plants.[1]

Employee disclosure and consultation

In October 1978, management and unions at Dundonald discussed a report produced by the Man-Made Fibre Working Party. This tripartite group consisted of senior representatives of government, trade unions and industry. Its report had pinpointed the three major sources of the UK industry's problems since 1973: the dramatic increase in the price of basic raw material, oil; the upsurge of imports; and a stagnant market for the final product. The same problems afflicted the entire European market.

Rising costs, and increased competition in a shrinking market, had knocked flat what had been a booming synthetic fibre industry in Britain and on the Continent. The abrupt emergence of an adverse business environment caught manufacturers off-guard. As demand slumped, they faced the additional problem of massive over-capacity in Western Europe.

The working party had found little reason for optimism, and had warned that 'problems arising from the cyclical nature of the industry will become more severe', and that consequently there would be 'a danger of idle capacity and redundancy'.[2]

Six months later, in April 1979, the group chairman announced that the company remained 'concerned' about the performance of its European nylon operations, and that it was in the process of completing 'a series of comprehensive studies aimed at examining all possible approaches for reducing the significant losses that are being generated by our nylon operations in Europe'. He added that the review of operation would be completed in early May, and that 'appropriate actions will be implemented as soon thereafter as practicable'.[3]

When trade union leaders at Dundonald read newspaper reports on the chairman's statement, they were convinced that the plant faced closure. Indeed, so certain were they that an action committee to oppose closure was formed during the first week of May.

On 9 May 1979, the British chairman of Monsanto's UK subsidiary announced the closure of the Dundonald plant, with the loss of all 830 jobs. Two key divestment factors were identified: Monsanto's unfavourable cost-competitive position, and its relatively small share of the nylon market. In the previous four years, Monsanto's UK subsidiary had suffered pre-tax losses of £8.9 million from nylon fibre operations.

The decision to close Dundonald had been taken only after a number of options had been considered, and after efforts had been made to stem the decline in the fiercely competitive man-made fibre market.

Dundonald employees received from the company a pamphlet, entitled, *Monsanto Ltd: Nylon Operations in the UK*. This outlined the economic rationale behind the decision to cease production in the UK. It explained that four options had been considered, and rejected: (1) continue with the status quo; (2) invest in new technology and equipment; (3) cut back operations and concentrate investment on the company's strongest products; and (4) maximize European production in the UK. None of these was considered a viable solution to the company's problems, and Monsanto felt it had no choice but to cease nylon production in Europe.[4]

According to the chairman of Monsanto's UK subsidiary at the time, the divestment decision had been made in London. His successor admits that it is unlikely that UK management could have reversed the decision without consulting the US parent, but trade union officials were denied access to US management, despite frequent requests.

According to one employee, Monsanto had been 'very underhand ... They have known for months they were closing the place'.[5] On 15 May the secretary of state for Scotland agreed to the shop stewards' suggestion that he should contact the parent company in St Louis, Missouri, to see whether the closure decision could be reversed.[6]

Two days later, a parent-company spokesman refuted the charge of local member of Parliament, Mr Lambie, that the US board had decided to close Dundonald. He said that the divestment decision had been made in London by UK subsidiary management.[7]

Further meetings took place between union officials and senior UK management to discuss Monsanto's decision. The plant closed on 27 July 1979, 78 days after the closure announcement of 9 May.

4.3 Akzo

Antrim

Background

The Dutch multinational Akzo has a divisional structure, with the 'Enka' subsidiary responsible for man-made fibre production. Enka is headquartered in West Germany. In 1961 it announced its plan to build a factory in the small town of Antrim, Northern Ireland, a small town with a population of just 3000. The Antrim plant was part of British Enkalon Ltd (referred to hereafter as 'Enkalon').

On opening in 1963, the plant produced only nylon textile yarn, but its product range was widened the following year. By 1966 the labour force exceeded 1000, and the future prosperity of plant and town alike seemed

Table 4.2 Performance Data on Enka, 1970–84
(G million)

Year	Sales	Operating income (loss)
1984	5035	302
1983	4526	151
1982	4359	(19)
1981	4678	33
1980	3782	(170)
1979	3852	74
1978	3567	10
1977	3598	(88)
1976	3804	(142)
1975	3707	(326)
1974	4528	223
1973	4398	390
1972	3798	231
1971	3840	371
1970	3561	325

Source: corporate accounts

assured. Antrim was designated a 'new town', and plans for its expansion to a potential population of 30 000 were undertaken by a steering committee hopeful of attracting further investment in Antrim and so reducing its dependence on Enkalon.[8]

By the early 1970s, the projected population growth was on course for reaching the target of 30 000 by 1981. However, Antrim had failed to attract new industry and the Ministry of Defence had closed its factory, leaving Enkalon the sole major employer in the area. The only consolation was that the plant's future appeared secure. The factory was profitable during its first ten years in operation—a minor loss was returned for only one year during that period—and the plant was expanded.[9]

Then, on 1 June 1974, disaster struck. The supplier of Antrim's raw materials—Nypro UK's Flixborough complex—was destroyed in a huge explosion at the plant. At the time, the basic raw material was in short supply, and Nypro's parent company, DSM of Holland, was unable to supply Enkalon. Production at Antrim continued, but only after raw materials had been purchased at inflated prices in the world market. Almost overnight, Antrim had become a high-cost operation. Costs were eventually cut back, but significantly, peak employment levels of over 3000 had been reached in early 1974. In the second half of the year a loss was returned. Antrim never again returned to profitability.

This blow to the Ulster plant coincided with the onset of an oil crisis which decimated Europe's man-made fibres industry. The cheap energy policy pursued by successive US governments had allowed American producers to flourish, and by 1979 they had cornered the European market with cheap imports. Enka's sales revenue dropped and net income was erratic (see Table 4.2).

Like other manufacturers in Europe, Enka was suffering from excess capacity and was struggling to preserve its share of a declining market. In 1981 the division rationalized its fibre operations at Breda, Holland, and Kassel, West Germany, Trade unionists on the Continent complained of the company's lack of employee disclosure and consultation. Akzo considered the criticism unjustified and presented evidence to the European Parliament to refute the unions' charge. In the same year, Enka announced the closure of its Antrim plant in Northern Ireland.

Employee disclosure and consultation

In July 1979, Enkalon's chief executive, a Dutchman, explained that Antrim would be streamlined in an attempt to stem losses by increasing productivity. This required 100 redundancies, but Enkalon and the Amalgamated Transport and General Workers Union (ATGWU) reached agreement on the procedure for voluntary redundancies.

Enka management still believed that, with further investment, the plant could, return to profitability, and in May 1980 a £33 million modernization programme for the 17-year-old plant was announced. However, this decision was rescinded later in the year owing to sterling's continued appreciation against the US dollar and the Dutch guilder.

On 27 June 1980, the Antrim site manager wrote to employees explaining that Enkalon had not faced such adverse market conditions since its arrival in 1963, and that short-time working would be introduced. He explained that 'the main objective is to preserve as many jobs as possible, under very difficult circumstances, and so the full co-operation of all employees is essential to the future of the Company.... Trade Union Representatives and all employees will be kept aware of the changes in the situation as and when these become known to Management'.[10]

Three days later, short-time working was introduced. Employees were told that this move was temporary, and that modernization would go ahead as planned.[11]

On 23 July 1980, Enkalon's published results for 1979 revealed a loss of £2 million. By early autumn it was apparent that Enka's management had underestimated the extent of the industry's problems, and those of Antrim in particular. Employees were advised of the gravity of the situation. Far from being a low-cost unit, Antrim had the highest production costs in the Enka group.[12]

By November the situation had deteriorated. Enkalon's chief executive, Mr Schierbeek, told shop stewards that closure was inevitable unless a 10 per cent reduction in production costs was achieved immediately. He outlined to shop stewards the measures necessary to meet this target. The management proposals had implications for all sections of the factory. The work-force rejected the proposals, confident that they had called the company's bluff.

Three days before Christmas, the group personnel manager met for consultation with Ballymena district secretary of the Amalgamated Transport and General Workers' Union (ATGWU), Mr Hanna. After the meeting he wrote to Mr Hanna confirming that there would be 150 redundancies at the plant. The following day, 23 December, a new agreement between the company and unions on 'Method of selection on personnel for redundancy' was reached which superceded all previous agreements. It stipulated that 'In principle every attempt will be made to effect the redundancy through volunteers. Where there is a shortfall, then nominations will be based upon overall company service, by Department.'

For Enkalon, 1980 had been a disastrous year. The strong pound and double-figure inflation rates and interest rates had compounded the company's problems. Sales revenue declined, and a loss of almost £10 million was incurred.

To stem this flow, on 19 January 1981, Enkalon announced that production of industrial yarns plus polyamide and polyester textiles would be significantly reduced, if not abandoned: 800 jobs would be lost, leaving a depleted work-force of 1100. In a detailed press release, Enkalon's chief executive outlined the problems facing Enka, and the uncertainty surrounding the Ulster plant.

A week later, Enkalon's personnel manager again wrote to Mr Hanna of the ATGWU, confirming that the company would be making a large number of its Antrim employees redundant. Having had its proposals for cost reduction rejected by employees, Enkalon announced that the factory would close on 19 June unless the government provided an £8.5 million subsidy.

On 20 May, the chief executive and chairman of Enkalon met union representatives, and explained that discussions with the Department of Commerce had lasted longer than the company had anticipated. The two sides had failed to reach agreement, and the Department had decided to commission a firm of management consultants to review the company's plans and request for financial assistance. The Department had received the consultants' report in early May, and discussions had continued throughout the month.[13]

The chief executive told employees that a conclusion would not be reached for several weeks, and that, accordingly, Enkalon was extending its deadline until August. The factory would now close on 31 August unless the £8.5 million financial aid package was forthcoming; regardless of the level of government assistance, 200 redundancies would be issued in June to workers in the textile section of the plant.

Despite massive unemployment in the province, the Department of Commerce refused fully to meet Enkalon's request, and on 15 July Enkalon announced that Antrim would close on 31 August. Enkalon revealed that 'the discussions with the Department of Commerce have not resulted in any viable proposal for the continuation of carpet yarn production' and, therefore, a decision had been taken to terminate carpet yarn production. The company statement said:[14]

> It is with great regret, particularly in view of the important social implications, and the positive attitude of all personnel during the past difficult months... [that] British Enkalon has no alternative but to close down the remainder of its fibre business.

Enkalon had asked for just £8.5 million and the editorial of the province's leading newspapers was highly critical of the government's failure to subsidize Enkalon with this 'not ... extraordinary amount'.[15]

Almost three weeks later, senior officials of the ATGWU led by its Northern Ireland secretary, John Freeman, met the chairman of Enka, Dr Hans-Gunther Zempelin. The possibility of retaining a reduced manufacturing facility was discussed, even though the closing-down process, which had begun on 15 July, was already at an advanced stage; the plant was virtually at a standstill, and raw material stocks were very low. But, as the Antrim site manager later explained, 'out of the blue ... came the chance to salvage some 800 jobs for a reduced production plant'.[16]

On 12 August a further meeting took place between Dr Zempelin and union officials at Enka's headquarters in Wuppertal. After the meeting,

Enka's chairman wrote to Mr Freeman confirming that the plant would continue production until 31 March 1982, at least. He informed Mr Freeman that the final decision would be based on an assessment in early 1982 of the plant's performance and market trends. In his letter, Dr Zempelin stressed that, 'from a business point of view, Enka has to prefer to see the closing down of Antrim as decided by the end of the month'; but, because of the social costs of closure, Enka was prepared 'to continue after the end of August on the basis of the alternative plan presented by the Union and the Work Force until March 31, 1982'. He explained that the Antrim plant would be appraised again in January/February 1982, but warned that 'a reconsideration of the closure decision is only possible if this reassessment leads to the conclusion that a positive result of the existing production programme can be achieved in the second quarter of 1982 and thereafter'.[17]

The company had agreed to accept the survival plan drawn up by the unions, and in return received a package of government aid totalling £1.5 million. Although the news was welcomed in most quarters, Sean Gibbons, secretary of the ATGWU's Enkalon branch, was highly critical of the officials in his own union for offering the company certain guarantees without first consulting the actual work-force which would have to honour them. He said that 'the union officials in the factory were kept completely in the dark. ... The wrong people are being praised for saving Enkalon. The union leaders got all the credit that should have gone to the workforce.'[18]

Details of the new survival plan, which would keep the plant in operation until March 1982 at least, were revealed to employees on 1 September. The plan required Antrim to manufacture several products in addition to carpet yarn. The site manager told employees that, if the plant consistently met its targets, and if the market situation improved sufficiently to break even in the second quarter, then 'it is possible that we could continue operating beyond March 1982'.[19] He said that the vitally important performance evaluation would be made during February 1982.

Over the next few months Antrim met its performance targets, but in his Christmas message to employees, Mr Schierbeek said that market conditions remained very unfavourable, and that it was these external factors 'which will eventually be the deciding influence'.[20] The employees at Enkalon, of course, had no control over these factors. It was clear that an up-turn in the man-made fibres market before February was necessary if the Antrim factory was to stay open.

On 5 February 1982 the site manager wrote to employees, reminding them that decision-day was approaching and that, 'in view of this continuing uncertainty and in consideration of your contractual right to notice, we are obliged to place you on notice to finish your employment on or by 30th April, 1982, i.e. the last working day or shift on or before that date', and added that 'this communication should be taken as your official letter of notice', although 'it is our sincere wish that the decision will be positive and that the factory will continue to provide employment after the end of March. Should this be the case, we will be in a position to rescind your notice without delay and notify you accordingly.'[21]

By the end of February, the Antrim plant's future had been decided. On 1 March, the Board of Enkalon announced the closure of the plant.

Over the following weeks, a series of telexes were exchanged between Antrim shop stewards and management at Enka's headquarters. On 29 March, Dr Zempelin confirmed that the decision was final.

The withdrawal of Enkalon signalled the departure of Antrim's largest employer. As a result, the town had the highest unemployment rate in Ulster, which itself had a rate double that for the UK as a whole.

But the story does not end there. In mid-June 1985, three years after the closure, Enka donated £1 million to establish the Enkalon Foundation 'to improve the quality of life in the Province and in recognition of the twenty years co-operation between the company and the people of Northern Ireland'.[22] Charitable projects in Ulster will receive £100 000 each year from the new trust fund.

The announcement followed a remark at the time of closure by the Communist secretary of the Amalgamated Transport and General Workers Union, Mr Freeman, to Dr Zempelin, the chairman of Enka, that £1 million would be appropriate compensation for the company to leave the people of Northern Ireland.

Mr Freeman, said:[23]

> I have never known such an immediate and sincere response to such a request, especially since the company had nothing to gain from it. It is further evidence of its concern for Northern Ireland and the value it places upon its reputation as a good employer, proven often to the people of Antrim.

Enka's gesture of goodwill was greatly appreciated in Ulster. The *Belfast Telegraph* leader writer commented:[24]

> Multinational companies are seldom noted for their generosity, particularly when they have nothing to gain, but the Dutch-owned ENKA group has proved a notable exception.
> ... The Publicity given to this gesture should alert others to their responsibilities, and give capitalism a better name. There is nothing more demoralising for workers, and the community they come from, to find out that a big employer has suddenly cut and run, with a minimum of redundancy payments.
> ... The gift is a tribute, too, to the Northern Ireland work-force, which had no responsibility for the market forces which brought about the closure.

4.4 Conclusions

Foreign divestment theory

In the mid-1960s, when Akzo established the Enkalon plant in Antrim and Monsanto opened its Dundonald facility, Europe offered location-specific advantages (i.e. a buoyant market and low costs) to producers of man-made fibres. Less than ten years later, these advantages had been dissipated. Demand was weak, and costs had soared owing to the escalating price of oil. Producers of man-made fibres in Europe became uncompetitive almost overnight, having lost ground to rivals in the USA, cushioned by a cheap energy policy. In Europe the consequences were all too apparent. Throughout the Continent modern plant was closed down, but the industry was still beset by excess capacity. The financial consequences were immediate and grave. The year 1975 was as disastrous as 1974 had been successful. It was to be only a mattern of time before Akzo and Monsanto disposed of their entire European man-made fibres manufacturing operations, including, of course, Antrim and Dundonald; but both firms were reluctant to abandon manufacturing facilities that were only ten years old, and so closure was postponed in the false hope that market conditions would improve.

It was seen in Chapter 2 that Boddewyn has identified three theoretical models to explain foreign divestment: condition-based theory, motivation-based theory, and precipitating-circumstances-based theory. There were no new men to prompt divestment in the two cases examined, so the third model does not apply to this case study. There were clearly sound motives for closing both plants, but, as was suggested in Chapter 2, poor subsidiary performance and losses merely signal the need for divestment: they hardly cause it. Thus the two closures examined here were in direct response to adverse changes in the business environment; i.e. the condition-based theory obtains.

Employee disclosure and consultation

Monsanto gave 78 days' notice (plus pay in lieu of notice), and therefore would appear to have done no more than meet the minimum legal requirements on employee disclosure and consultation. The Dutch MNC, Akzo, instead conformed to the spirit of the law. Enkalon and Enka—Akzo's subsidiaries—more than satisfied UK legal requirements of redundancy notice. Employees at Antrim were entitled to at least 90 days' notice of redundancy: they in fact received 12–14 months' notice, having first been notified in early 1981.

However, length of notification of redundancy alone hardly seems a satisfactory measure of employee disclosure and consultation. Trade union representatives want an opportunity to discuss the merits of divestment decisions with the actual decision-makers. They are often deprived of this, and so-called 'consultations' are reduced to haggling over redundancy payments with managers powerless to reconsider, let alone reverse, the closure decision.

Meetings with host-country unions and parent-company management may not avert closures, but they can nevertheless prove beneficial to both parties. They allow union officials to claim that all options to save the plant have been exhausted, and to enter redundancy negotiations rather than engaging in mere face-saving opposition to job losses. MNCs get the opportunity to project a wholesome image of caring capitalism, rather than one of callous profit-maximizing and disinterest in the welfare of the community. Direct union contact with foreign decision-makers was crucial in the Antrim case, and both community and company reaped the benefits.

The foreign divestment decision process of Akzo's subsidiary Enka is unique among those examined in this thesis. Management at Enka's head-quarters in Germany not only agreed to hold consultations with British trade unionists, but as a result of these they *revoked* the original foreign divestment decision. The final decision to close Antrim was taken only after a reappraisal of market demand confirmed that conditions had deteriorated further during the seven-month extension period. No one in Ulster could have been shocked by the closure of the Enkalon plant.

Akzo, a Dutch MNC, and its subsidiaries acted considerately throughout the closing process at Antrim. When the firm subsequently donated £1 million for the benefit of Ulster, its reputation was further enhanced and the gesture evoked the highest praise from the province's top trade unionist.

The extent of centralized decision-making assumed in the Vredeling Proposals is apparently slightly at odds with Akzo's decision-making structure. Mr Schierbeek, CEO of Enkalon, was empowered with a degree of authority uncommon in subsidiary management of MNCs. For example, he acted independently, he says, when issuing the threat to close Antrim in 1980. He therefore had decision-making powers far in excess of those that Vredeling attributes to subsidiary management. He did not merely implement parent company decisions: he shaped them.

Akzo's conduct in the Enkalon case appears beyond reproach. Perhaps it is significant that not only is Dutch labour legislation recognized as one of the most progressive among EC countries, and that the Vredeling Proposals borrowed heavily from it, but that Mr Vredeling is himself a Dutchman.

References

1. Monsanto, *Annual Report*, 1978.
2. Monsanto, *Nylon Operations in the United Kingdom*, 9 May 1979.
3. Monsanto, Public Relations Department, Brussels, press release, 25 April 1979.
4. Monsanto, 9 May 1979, op. cit.
5. 'Repair work needed', *Glasgow Herald*, 10 May 1979.
6. 'Younger agrees on plea to Monsanto', *Glasgow Herald*, 16 May 1979.
7. 'Government offer on Monsanto closure', *The Scotsman*, 15 May 1979.
8. 'For good or bad, Antrim has built around Enkalon', *Ballymena Observer*, 23 July 1981.
9. Ibid.
10. P. L. Lemmens, Antrim site manager, 27 June 1980.
11. 'Short-time working at Enkalon' *Ballymena Guardian*, 3 July 1980.

12. R. Schierbeek, former chief executive officer of British Enkalon Ltd; telephone interview with author, 25 February 1985.
13. 'Enkalon discussions taking longer than expected', *Ballymena Guardian*, 28 May 1981.
14. Joint announcement by AK20 NV and British Enkalon Ltd, *British Enkalon*, 25 May 1981.
15. *Belfast Telegraph*; quoted in *Ballymena Observer*, 23 July 1981; see n. 8 above.
16. P. L. Lemmens, Antrim site manager, 1 September 1981.
17. H. G. Zempelin, chairman of Enka, letter of 12 August 1981 to John Freeman, Northern Ireland secretary, Amalgamated Transport General Workers Union.
18. 'Unions sold out Enkalon', *Ballymena Observer*, 27 August 1981.
19. P. L. Lemmens, Antrim site manager, 1 September 1981.
20. 'So far, so good on Enkalon Jobs', *Ballymena Observer*, 23 December 1981.
21. P. L. Lemmens, Antrim site manager, letter of 5 February 1982 to employees.
22. Inter-City Bureaux, press release.
23. Ibid.
24. 'Parting-gift', *Belfast Telegraph*, 18 June 1985.

5
The domestic appliance/consumer electronics industry

5.1 Introduction

This chapter reviews three plant closures in three of the UK's home countries. In 1979 the US multinational Singer announced the closure of its huge sewing machine plant in Scotland. The following year Northern Ireland suffered another body-blow when the German MNC Grundig decided to close its Belfast plant with the loss of 1000 jobs. And in 1981, Hoover chose to continue floorcare equipment production at its Cambuslang factory at the expense of its Perivale, London, plant. These three closures involved a direct loss of 5000 jobs, but at their peak the factories had a much larger labour force than this figure suggests; for example, Singer's Clydebank plant alone once employed more than 16 000 people.[1]

Unlike the other industrial case studies, the three firms examined in this chapter manufactured quite different products: Singer, sewing machines; Grundig, radio cassettes; Hoover, vacuum-cleaners and laundry equipment. This variation in product precludes the inclusion of a general review of market conditions. Instead, each case is dealt with separately.

This chapter serves to underline variations in the corporate divestment process. The Singer Clydebank plant was gradually frozen out of the US corporation's European operations over a period of twenty years. This very gradual rundown is mirrored in the review of the foreign divestment process. On the other hand, the closure of Grundig's Dunmurry plant was so unexpected that the actual closure announcement was the first public indication of a divestment strategy. (In virtually all other plant closures examined in these case studies, it is possible to detect the onset of a divestment process.) The abruptness of Grundig's closure announcement is reflected in the brief consideration it is afforded here. Hoover, like Singer, informed employees of its difficulties, and its decision to close Perivale was hardly a shock to its work-force.

From a corporate perspective, Hoover appears to have handled its divestment process with consummate skill. The effect of its disclosure policy was to play one plant off against the other—Perivale versus Cambuslang. Union officials at each were thus compelled to argue the case for closing the other facility. This divide-and-conquer strategy may have been purely fortuitous, but examples exist (e.g. Goodyear in Drumchapel) where MNCs have succeeded in achieving highly desirable results by frankness. Perhaps trade union officials should cease to attribute these results to luck on the part of MNCs, and consider the possibility that the unions have been outsmarted.

5.2 Singer

Founded in 1850, Singer had become by 1867 the unchallenged world leader of the sewing machine industry. In the same year, it chose Glasgow, in Scotland, as the location for its first foreign manufacturing plant. Buoyant demand forced a transferral to new premises in Glasgow in 1872, and again in 1884, when it moved to its purpose-built plant at Clydebank, a few miles west of the city.

By 1946 Singer was no longer enjoying a monopoly of the sewing machine market, and competition was intense. Despite this, the US multinational continued to market machines of Victorian design, manufactured with nineteenth-century tools, in similarly outdated buildings. In 1957 sewing machines accounted for 94 per cent of the company's total sales, with virtually all domestic machines being sold in Singer's own retail outlets. Singer was therefore highly dependent on a single product, and one that it had failed to develop. This alone made it very vulnerable to the competition that was emerging in the *domestic* sewing machine market, and the condition was exacerbated by the location of virtually all of its production facilities in high-wage countries, with almost half of its machines being produced in Clydebank.

Competition came first from European sewing machine manufacturers, but this was followed in the early 1950s by competition from Japan, which had stormed world markets with low-cost domestic machines, making substantial inroads into Singer's markets.

Before the Second World War, Japan had produced virtually no sewing machines and Singer had a 90 per cent share of the Japanese market. But in 1945, US General Douglas MacArthur, responsible for rebuilding the war-torn Japanese economy, decided that the vanquished Japanese should produce sewing machines instead of munitions. Singer was forbidden to re-enter the Japanese market. The irony was that Singer patents and plans were provided, along with US capital investment, to establish the industry in Japan. By the 1950s Japan had made great progress, and by 1957 over 300 companies were producing over 2 million domestic machines. The Japanese firms succeeded where their European counterparts had failed. Singer's US market share for domestic machines plummeted from 66 per cent in 1950 to 33 per cent in 1957, and to make matters worse, that same year saw a sharp decline in the US market. Singer's market share fell to approximately 35 per cent in most foreign markets.

The decline of Singer in the *domestic* sewing machine market was in marked contrast with the company's continued dominance of the *industrial* sewing machine market: in 1957 Singer still held 44 per cent of the world market for industrial machines. The poor performance in the domestic sewing machine markets was mainly responsible for Singer's 25 per cent drop in profits between 1951 and 1957.

It was against this background that Donald Kircher was appointed president of Singer in 1958. His priority was the revitalization of the sewing machine industry. This demanded major changes at Clydebank.

Clydebank

Background

By 1960, the Clydebank plant had been in operation for almost eighty years. Mr Kircher was aware that the Scottish factory as it stood was a monument to Singer's period of masterly inactivity—a relic of the nineteenth century. Machine tools bought in 1867 for the opening of Singer's first Scottish plant were still in use at Clydebank during the 1960s. Major changes were necessary if Singer and its Clydebank facility were to compete successfully with the newly equipped Japanese rivals. The plant was to be reorganized and revitalized.

In 1961 a Forward Planning Unit (FPU) was established. Staffed by Americans from the parent company, its task was to pinpoint and remedy the defects within the factory, devise a campaign of modernization, and reduce costs by increasing productivity.

The FPU decided immediately that substantial investment would be forthcoming. A new building was erected, and by late 1964 all domestic sewing machine production had been transferred to this modern unit. This coincided with organizational change at Clydebank. In July 1964, the factory was basically divided into two groups, the Consumer Products Group (CPG) and the Industrial Products Group (IPG). The CPG manufactured only domestic machines, the IPG only industrial models. As a result, Singer could better assess the efficiency of the Clydebank plant.

Mr Kircher had also recognized the dangers involved in Singer's excessive reliance on its nineteenth-century Scottish plant. He decided that this should change:[2]

> We are scaling down Clydebank somewhat by transferring one line to Bonnieres. Clydebank will still be our largest factory, but the others will be much closer in size than in the past.

Clydebank and the French plant at Bonnieres were to produce 'middle-of-the-line' domestic sewing machines, but demand in Europe and the USA was increasingly for either the best or the cheapest models, produced at Karlsruhe, West Germany, and Monza, Italy, respectively. Therefore the Scottish and French plants were producing domestic machines with the least market potential. Bonnieres had a great advantage over Clydebank, however, as it was closely integrated with Monza, Karlsruhe and Wurselen (also in Germany): the closure of any one of these plants would have upset production in at least two of the others. Clydebank, in its singular self-sufficiency, was more vulnerable to closure.

Between 1961 and 1965, £7.8 million was invested in Clydebank, most of it in the CPG which continued to produce models designed for the European and American markets. During the same period, investment in the IPG was almost negligible. This appeared ominous to the local work-force, which had been informed of a new factory being built at Blankenloch in Germany. Blankenloch, which produced only industrial machines, opened in 1967. The IPG at Clydebank remained housed in a six-storey Edwardian building which was unsuitable for manufacturing any sewing machines, let alone heavy cumbersome models. From 1964 on, the IPG was trapped in a 'Catch-22' situation: unless a profitable position was reached, there would be no investment; unless there was investment, a profitable position could not be reached. As early as May 1965, employees were warned by local management that the IPG's future was uncertain, as it was mainly responsible for the deterioration in Clydebank's financial performance. During the period 1962–71, the Scottish plant made a profit of only £4.6 million, and there was considerable fluctuation in profits from year to year (see Table 5.1).

By the early 1970s, the US and European markets were in decline, and the closure of Clydebank drew nearer. An indication of the importance of those markets is that in 1975 they accounted for 85 per cent of the factory's domestic sewing machine output and 43 per cent of its industrial machine output. The growing Third World markets were now being served by new plants which Singer had opened in the developing countries. The company was clearly reducing the strategic importance of its European operations, especially Clydebank. Despite management having given assurances that

Table 5.1 Performance data on the Singer Manufacturing Company Ltd (i.e. the Clydebank factory) (£'000)

Year	Sales	Pre-tax profits	Post-tax profits	% return on investment
1971	18 445	1312.0	738.0	7.7
1970	17 219	1111.0	766.0	8.3
1969	19 463	2516.0	2516.0	20.0
1968	15 478	1388.0	1388.0	13.5
1967	11 826	(183.0)	(249.0)	negative
1966	n.a.	(117.0)	13.0	negative
1965	n.a.	(889.0)	(889.0)	negative
1964	n.a.	58.1	58.1	0.7
1963	n.a.	246.8	246.8	2.9
1962	n.a.	74.5	52.7	0.9

Source: company accounts

there would be no compulsory redundancies, the plant's labour force was cut from 15 866 to 6400 during the decade 1960–70, largely in response to Mr Kircher's decision to reduce Clydebank's production capacity, and therefore its level of output.

In 1975, the IPG was still producing machines in conditions that rendered profit-making well-nigh impossible; indeed, this group had not shown a single profitable year in the 1970s. The closure of the IPG seemed imminent; but instead, Singer announced that Blankenloch would be closed and production transferred to Clydebank, thereby creating 500 jobs. There was sound logic behind this apparent surprise decision: closing Clydebank's IPG would have involved considerable losses in write-offs, whereas the modern German plant could be sold. The transfer of plant was completed within a year and was fraught with difficulties.

Meanwhile, the company's troubles were not confined to Clydebank. By 1975 Singer's debts had escalated, its diversification policy was in tatters, and the company's banks had lost confidence in Kircher. In December 1975, Joseph Flavin, then chief executive vice-president of Xerox, replaced Mr Kircher as president.

Singer was highly dependent on its sewing-related products, and ironically, the company's *domestic* sewing machine operations proved highly profitable in 1975. The CPG at Clydebank did not contribute to this success, while the IPG at Clydebank was largely responsible for the corporation's worldwide industrial sewing machine operations' reported loss of $10 million. The Clydebank factory was a massive drain on corporate resources. Its strategic role had been greatly reduced during Kircher's reign, and the company was no longer dependent upon it.

In 1976 Singer again made a profit—$74.2 million—and in 1977 profits rose to $94.2 million (see Table 5.2). The Scottish plant, however, remained the thorn in Singer's flesh. Clydebank, which had returned a loss of £2.6 million in 1975 (the IPG alone lost £2.2 million), lost £680 000 in 1976. In

Table 5.2 Performance data for the Singer Company, 1973–80

Year	Sales ($'000)	Net income ($'000)	No. of employees
1980	2 786 000	38 100	71 000
1979	2 598 100	(92 300)	77 000
1978	2 469 200	62 800	81 000
1977	2 294 300	94 200	86 000
1976	2 125 500	74 200	85 000
1975	2 568 000	(451 900)	98 000
1974	2 661 700	(10 100)	111 000
1973	2 527 600	94 500	122 000

Source: N. Hood and S. Young, *Multinationals in Retreat*, Edinburgh University Press, 1982.

1977 Larry Neely, an American, replaced John Wotherspoon as managing director, with Mr Wotherspoon being made chairman of Singer UK. In that year Clydebank's loss was $2.8 million, and this could be attributed directly to the IPG, which reported a staggering loss of $8 million. The CPG, on the other hand, which had received some investment, made a profit of $5.2 million.

Later in 1977, Mr Flavin visited Clydebank for the first time, on a fact-finding mission. Local management prepared a comprehensive report showing that, despite a lack of investment, there had been a significant increase in productivity since 1967. Given the age of the plant's capital equipment, this was quite an achievement. As of November 1976, the total number of machines in the factory was 7512, of which 862 were over 50 years old, 128 were over 75 years old and 7 were over 100 years old.

As a result of the 1972–79 slump in domestic sewing machine sales, Singer had 'serious over-capacity' in Europe and the USA, and the *Singer Shareholder News Letter* produced for the third quarter of 1979 suggested that the first step of a 'restructuring programme' to solve this problem was the closure of Clydebank.[3] The CPG of the company's oldest factory in Europe had the lowest productivity of Singer's 28 plants, and, unlike the others in Europe, it could be closed without disrupting production elsewhere. Clydebank was an anachronism.

Management recognized that productivity in the IPG was low and costs were high, but instead of providing investment, expected the workers to find a solution. Even the CPG, which had received almost all of the £10 million invested at Clydebank, was in 1976 still heavily dependent on tools that had been in use during the 1950s. This lack of investment and a demoralized work-force compounded the CPG's low productivity. As the labour force contracted, many of the remaining workers believed that the company had already decided to close the factory.

By the end of 1977, it was hard to believe that the Clydebank factory had once been the hub of the Singer empire. Closure seemed inevitable.

Employee disclosure and consultation

On 13 March 1978, the factory convener and his deputy travelled to London to meet national officers of the trade unions represented at Clydebank. Two days later, these officials discussed the factory's future with the then secretary of state for Scotland, who indicated that government money was available, but that so far Singer had not approached the government. A few days later, the Labour Party in Scotland held its annual conference. A lobby of shop stewards from the Clydebank plant attended to convey the gravity of the situation at the factory. They discussed the matter with the then prime minister, Mr Callaghan, who promised to raise the matter with President Carter during their forthcoming meeting in America.

On 22 March, trade union representatives met Ed Keehn, president of

Singer's European Division, Sewing Products Group. According to the unions, Mr Keehn had agreed to the shop stewards request[4]

> that, prior to any decisions being made relative to the future of the Clydebank factory and its total workforce, and in light of the fact that Management is currently conducting a World Wide Survey of its products manufacturing base and selling outlets, the Trade Unions should be given an opportunity to—
> (a) examine the draft proposals arising from this report,
> (b) be given the opportunity to view the alternatives contained within the report, as these alternatives may affect the Clydebank plant, and
> (c) be given a commitment that no decisions will be taken by Singer Corporate Management on the results of this survey prior to the foregoing procedures being carried out.

The statement does not reveal, however, that during this meeting Mr Keehn assured the union delegation that the Clydebank plant would not be closed.

In the first six months of 1978, Singer had reported a loss of $3.4 million on industrial sewing machines, and Clydebank's IPG, which produced half of all Singer industrial machines, was largely responsible. In early April a union delegation met Mr Keehn, who informed the shop stewards that Mr Flavin had agreed to visit Britain in June to discuss the factory's future with government ministers and union leaders.

On 22 June, Mr Flavin announced his plans for the Clydebank factory in a letter to its employees. He revealed that Singer was prepared to spend about £8 million in updating operations, restructuring the work-force, and tooling for a new household sewing machine in order to give Clydebank 'a vital new role in developed markets'.[5] On the other hand, he wrote, it was necessary to streamline consumer sewing operations. The IPG was to be phased out over five years, by which time the factory would employ around 2000 people. Mr Flavin stressed that 'it is our belief that this course of action and no other can ensure the continuation of the Clydebank factory'.[6]

According to some reports, the head office had wanted to close the entire plant, and only the intervention of Prime Minister Callaghan had persuaded Singer to retain the CPG. In many respects, the company's decision not to close Clydebank was a surprise, but just five days after Mr Flavin's warning, the work-force overwhelmingly supported the following resolution:[7]

> This meeting of Singer workers totally rejects the company's proposals to run down Industrial Sewing Machine Products, and calls for the reversal of the present company policy by immediate cash investment to achieve:
> (a) Continuation of all Industrial Products.
> (b) Maximum job opportunity in the short term and long term at Singer, Clydebank.

Only 'about ten' workers voted against the resolution.[8]

Two days later, the unions agreed that the services of professionals should be called upon to advise on a viable alternative for the factory. It was decided at a Factory Committee meeting on 24 July that a firm called PA Management Consultants should be hired. The unions hoped that the government would completely finance the project. By early August, the factory convener was able to report that he had received a letter from the Private Secretary to the Prime Minister, Gregor MacKenzie, which stated that, if the unions put up £25 000, the Scottish Development Agency would provide the other £50 000. The Factory Committee unanimously decided to accept this offer. The unions raised their share by a levy of 50p per worker per week for a period of ten weeks. According to the minutes of the union meeting held on 12 September, documentary evidence was produced which indicated that the company was already in the process of phasing out the IPG—this to be completed by 1980, and not 1981, as had appeared in Flavin's plan. When confronted, management denied that it was breaking the agreement not to implement the phasing-out plan until the unions had had some time to consider a viable alternative.

While PA carried on preparing the report on how to save jobs, the workers themselves were apathetic. One shop steward stated that only 30 per cent of his members wanted to fight for their jobs.[9] During the first week of October, the factory convenor informed the Factory Committee that a director of the Scottish Development Agency had been informed that, 'if quick decisions were not made, then there was a danger the company would possibly close down the whole factory'.[10] Later that month it was revealed that all Singer's European plants, with the exception of Clydebank, had obtained an increase in orders for domestic machines in 1979, whereas Clydebank had fewer orders than in 1978.

Early in November, the union-commissioned consultants' report was submitted to Singer's management. It outlined the alternative strategy, which retained a reduced Industrial Products facility at Clydebank, provided employment for 3000 people (compared with Singer proposals for 2250), and envisaged development, over the following year or two, of an enhanced Industrial Products range to secure the future and possibly generate further employment.

At the end of November, Singer replied to the factory trade union leaders on PA Consultants' alternative strategy. It agreed to continue manufacturing two industrial models and thus save 335 jobs. This would involve a further investment of between £1 million and £2 million beyond the estimated £8 million. The unions were 'bitterly disappointed' that Singer had not accepted the alternative strategy in full, and 'at this juncture are rejecting the company's proposals'.[11] The plant's US manager remained convinced that, 'if all the parties co-operate to the fullest, ... there can be a future at Clydebank'.[12] He did warn, however, that the plant had 15 months to prove itself or face closure.

On 8 December Singer revised its offer, and now stated that, 'subject to external finance of the estimated order £2 to £4 million becoming available on terms acceptable to Singer', production of another two industrial machine models and related spares would continue, thereby supporting 165 jobs in addition to the 335 previously offered.[13] Three days later, Mr Keehn told the factory's 130 shop stewards that Singer had reluctantly agreed to accept the government's offer of the finance necessary to retain a reduced IPG, only because the company wanted to continue producing domestic machines at Clydebank. He also warned them that, if the workers rejected this latest proposal, Singer would close down the whole factory. The factory's deputy convener then called on the shop stewards to accept, in principle, the company's proposals, and to advise the workers to do the same; 74 shop stewards backed his recommendation, but as many as 54 voted against it.

On 13 December, the workers rejected, by about two to one, the shop stewards' recommendation 'to accept in principle the company's proposals'. The factory deputy convener warned that rejection would lead to closure; he was booed by the workers, whose attitude was typified by the one who said, 'Singer management have held a pistol to our heads; let them pull the trigger'.[14]

A company statement from the US headquarters was issued saying that Singer was 'extremely disappointed and apprehensive about the implications of the vote taken today by manual workers in Clydebank, Scotland to reject the proposal of union leadership to implement a plan designed to save its sewing products factory there'. Mr Keehn explained that[15]

> This was hoped to have become a solution to benefit everyone concerned, including the Clydebank community as a whole. It is unfortunate that the workforce has chosen to be so cavalier in its first reaction.
> Without the endorsement by the total workforce the plan to save Clydebank cannot be successful. And without the plan the Company can see no practical way to continue operations there much less invest one penny more in the plant.
> Although the financial impact on the total company of the plant being closed would be significant, it is a step the Company will take if the membership causes it.
> We are hopeful that more responsible consideration will be given to the leadership's call for support of the plan. It would be tragic to force the closing of the plant on the eve of such an enlightened solution to the situation there; a solution developed in an atmosphere of almost unprecedented cooperation between management, labour leaders and government.

The shop stewards realized that closure was likely unless the manual workers accepted the company's plan, but saving the factory was not uppermost in many workers' minds. The majority were apparently urging their representatives to restrict negotiations to securing favourable redundancy payments.[16]

Early in 1979, at a meeting held in London at the request of Singer, Mr Keehn informed a trade union delegation that Mr Flavin's original plan would be implemented immediately. The trade unionists asked Mr Keehn for a seven-day extension before implementing the plan; they argued that the manual workers were now ready to approve the modified plan which would save an extra 500 jobs. Their argument proved persuasive, and during a break in the proceedings Mr Keehn telephoned US headquarters and gained parent-company approval of the unions' proposal. The company agreed to give the manual workers a second chance. There was to be another vote a week later when, once again, the workers would be asked to accept the same motion that they had rejected in December. On 12 January, the acting factory convener instructed the stewards 'to go back to their members and impress upon them that this is their last chance to save the factory'.[17] Five days later employees voted, this time two to one in favour of the motion.

Four months later, on 4 May, the Conservatives won the general election, with Mrs Thatcher replacing Mr Callaghan as prime minister. On the same day, Mr Keehn announced that the Clydebank factory faced closure unless the unions agreed to accept the company's new pay plan. A settlement was reached on 14 May, but the factory's financial problems remained. In the first six months of 1979, Clydebank had made a loss of £6 million and the order books were very low. In June a four-day week was introduced, but losses continued to mount. By August the plant had run up losses of $14.25 million. The £8 million investment promised by the company had still not materialized, although all the conditions laid down by Mr Flavin had been met. Speculation was rife that the company had decided to close Clydebank. When Labour had lost the general election in May, perhaps Singer felt it was no longer constrained to honour the promises made to Labour MPs to remain in Clydebank.

On 12 October, Singer announced that the Scottish plant would close in June 1980, with the loss of 3000 jobs.

5.3   Grundig

The origins of Grundig date from 1927, when a small radio shop was opened in a small town near Nuremburg, Germany. From these humble origins, Max Grundig created a business empire which won renown for its high-quality audio and video equipment.

In 1960 Grundig opened its first foreign plant, at Dunmurry, on the outskirts of Belfast, in Northern Ireland. The plant produced radio recorders and stereo equipment, but it could not compete with rival producers from the Far East, which had much lower labour costs. Although both management and shop-floor workers had realized the threat posed by the success of producers from the Far East, Dunmurry's future did not seem to be in jeopardy.

Dunmurry

Background

The Dunmurry plant consistently returned profits until 1978 and 1979, when losses of approximately £0.5 million and £1.0 million respectively were reported.

During a rare industrial dispute, in March 1979, Grundig threatened to close Dunmurry and transfer production to Germany, where (as in France) a rationalization of production facilities had begun in January of that year, resulting in large job losses. The strike was quickly settled, but just a year later Grundig announced its shock decision to close the Dunmurry plant.

The media in the UK have a tendency to present all plant closure announcements as sudden, unexpected 'shocks'. It can be seen from the cases presented in this book that many foreign-owned plant closures could have been, and indeed were, anticipated by employees. In a few cases, however, workers were genuinely stunned to hear of their employers decision to close the plant. This was certainly true of those at Dunmurry.

Employee disclosure and consultation

On 30 June 1980, the director of personnel at Grundig's German head-quarters arrived in Belfast to meet an anxious local management team who were anticipating redundancies, but certainly not closure.[18]

In retrospect, their gloomy predictions can be seen to have erred on the side of optimism; for they were informed that Dunmurry would close on 10 October with the loss of all 1000 jobs. Even senior plant management was taken aback by Grundig's decision. Within the space of one hour, local management and workers alike heard, for the first time, that the German parent company had decided to cease all production at Dunmurry.

The foreign divestment decision was based on the Ulster plant's failure to produce goods capable of competing on a cost basis with those manufactured in the Far East. A gradual rundown of the plant was out of the question because it would have necessitated operating at a sub-optimal level, thereby increasing production costs. As it was, Dunmurry's best was not viable.

It was for these reasons that full production was maintained until the day of closure, and why Grundig pulled out of Dunmurry almost as soon as was legally possible—101 days after its closure announcement.

5.4 Hoover

In 1908, Mr William H. Hoover formed the Electric Suction Sweeper Company. He had foreseen the market potential of a practical vacuum-cleaner, and his assessment proved correct. Business boomed, and international production began in 1911 with the opening of a manufacturing facility at Ontario, Canada, which exported to the UK. In 1922 the company was renamed the Hoover Company. By the 1930s the company had an unchallenged brand image in Britain—where people already spoke of 'hoovering' their carpets. The Canadian plant's capacity was being stretched beyond its limits, and it was decided to establish a factory in the UK. Production commenced at Perivale, London, in 1932.

Further plants were opened in the UK—at Cambuslang, near Glasgow, in

Table 5.3   Performance data on the Hoover Company, 1970–81

Year	Sales ($'000)	Assets ($'000)	Net income ($'000)	No. of employees
1981*	749 919	449 721	(18 778)	n.a.
1980	830 465	532 367	30 048	20 081
1979	754 324	491 091	39 263	21 523
1978	691 817	474 350	24 648	22 587
1977	590 740	425 981	23 462	23 370
1976	571 913	391 248	6 838	22 886
1975	593 747	391 489	11 903	23 713
1974	502 731	384.617	8 711	27 452
1973	534 655	399 076	33 035	27 947
1972	458 415	346 123	29 514	25 499
1971	402 282	309 094	21 673	22 578
1970	346 686	275 522	17 860	22 602

Source: * company accounts; N. Hood and S. Young, *Multinationals in Retreat: The Scottish Experience*, Edinburgh University Press, 1982, p. 98.

1946 and at Merthyr Tydfil, in South Wales, in 1948. Hoover PLC, the UK subsidiary, had wholly owned subsidiaries in Austria, Portugal, Australia, South Africa and the Scandinavian countries. It also has a 50 per cent share in Hoover (Holland) BV, a holding company for operating units in Holland, Belgium, France, Germany, Italy and Switzerland.

As with Singer, Hoover's diversification policy of the 1960s–1970s was a failure. Net income plummeted from a peak of over $33 million in 1973 to just under $7 million in 1976 (see Table 5.3). This poor performance had led to changes in top management, with Merle Rawson being appointed chief executive officer in 1974.

After the mid-1970s, the market in industrialized countries for floor-care and laundry equipment became increasingly competitive, as major new players emerged to challenge Hoover and other well established manufacturers of white goods. Electrolux of Sweden had already expanded rapidly by a series of astute acquisitions.

Hoover's performance was determined largely by its European operations. The UK market alone accounted for one-third of total parent-company sales, and UK employees accounted for 60 per cent of total employment in the Hoover group.

Perivale

Background

By the late 1970s, Hoover's UK subsidiary faced an increasingly hostile business environment. It served markets that had been swamped by cheap

Table 5.4 Performance data on Hoover's UK subsidiary, Hoover PLC, 1972–81

Year	Sales (£m)	Net profit before tax (£m)	Ave. no. of UK employees ('000)
1981	201.1	(31.8)	9.8*
1980	206.7	(2.7)	10.2*
1979	203.7	1.9	11.8
1978	212.1	5.3	13.5
1977	191.0	12.2	13.5
1976	180.0	17.0	13.3
1975	162.9	20.7	14.2
1974	113.8	4.2	15.8
1973	121.0	24.0	14.9
1972	98.4	19.5	13.1

* At year-end 1980, UK employment was 10 224; by year-end 1981, the figure had fallen to 6854.

Source: company records; N. Hood and S. Young, *Multinationals in Retreat: The Scottish Experience*, Edinburgh University Press, 1982, p. 99.

imports from the Iron Curtain countries, and its share of the UK vacuum-cleaner market fell from 50 per cent in 1978 to 40 per cent in 1980, while Electrolux maintained a steady 32 per cent.

As Hoover's unit sales fell, the company's three UK plants cut back on production. Operating below capacity demanded a significant reduction in the numbers employed. Failure to respond earlier to changing market conditions had taken its toll on Hoover PLC. Profits fell by almost 50 per cent between 1972 and 1977 despite the fact that during the same period turnover increased from £98 million to £191 million (see Table 5.4). Whereas previously profits were about 20 per cent of sales revenue, by 1978 that figure had fallen to 3 per cent; and return on investment had fallen from 35 to 7 per cent. Added to this, the company had a cash-flow problem; the group balance sheet had shown over £22 million in liquid funds at the beginning of 1977, but by 1980 it showed net borrowings of £15 million.[19]

All of these problems came to a head, and a post-tax loss of £4.1 million was reported in 1980—the first loss since becoming a public company in 1937. In an effort to restore profitability, 900 workers were made redundant—400 at Cambuslang, 300 at Merthyr Tydfil and 200 at Perivale. The erratic performance of the UK subsidiary was hardly surprising, given the low productivity, poor labour relations, weak marketing, low investment and unresponsive management. Remedial action was required.

Even more ominous for UK employees was the revelation that the US board had decided to reduce the strategic importance of British operations:[20]

We expect 1981 to be a difficult year, especially in the first half, as we continue to restructure the United Kingdom manufacturing operations. This action will incur one-time costs, but will help increase productivity and reduce ongoing costs.

Having suffered a loss in 1980, the parent company exerted pressure on the UK subsidiary to reduce costs and return to profitability before the end of 1981. In the UK, 6000 jobs had been lost since 1975, and it was believed that more would be announced by the subsidiary's new managing director, Peter Goode, who had been appointed in mid-August 1981.[21]

Employee disclosure and consultation

By the late summer of 1981, many employees believed that Mr Goode would close Cambuslang in order to reduce the UK labour force. The number employed at the Scottish facility had already been halved since the mid-1970s, and the plant was now operating at less than two-thirds capacity. The media speculated that Perivale had a secure future, but the London factory's work-force had, for a number of years, expressed grave concern over job security.

Although, UK management was unwilling to provide Perivale stewards with certain information (i.e. on profitability of Perivale's products), the minutes of meetings between management and union officials confirm that the workers' representatives regularly received detailed information regarding the performance of UK operations, and of Perivale in particular.

For example, on 18 August 1980 meetings took place at Hoover's three UK factories to explain to shop stewards the difficult situation facing the company. Four months later, similar meetings were convened at which shop stewards were informed that some redundancies had already been made—short-time working was necessary, and inventories had been reduced—but that the company was still £1 million over target; net borrowings had risen from £11.2 million in June to more than £20 million in December; a loss of £1.6 million had been incurred on a turnover of £51.3 million in the third quarter; a trading profit of only £862 000 on a turnover of £152 million had been reported in the first nine months of 1980.[22]

The next meeting with Perivale's Joint Consultative Committee (JCC) was held on 4 March 1981. Mr Bristow, director, met with employees' representatives. He presented a gloomy picture. In 1980 the turnover of Hoover PLC had risen by only £3 million (less than 1.5 per cent), and the UK subsidiary reported its first ever loss. Moreover, despite redundancies and short-time working, stock worth £56 million was held at the end of the year. According to Mr Bristow, this was[23]

some £20 million above our requirement to operate the business normally. Because of this excess we had to borrow money, and at the year end we were borrowing £13 million and we paid £2 million in interest throughout the year. So, although our short-time working was necessary, it did not go far enough to effect any real improvement.

We have entered 1981 with high stocks, a continuing recession and an increasing overdraft. Even the confidence of our shareholders has been shaken, not only by the first loss on record but also because their dividend has been slashed to half the level of previous years.

Our continuation of short-time working in January and February has helped, but as with last year it is not enough to keep the Company viable and guarantee any real improvement in our situation.

There is no sign that the recession in the United Kingdom is abating, and the high value of our currency makes it almost impossible to increase exports of our products to other countries where inflation is lower. Meanwhile, our stocks will continue to increase our borrowings and pay higher interest charges. Unless we take concerted action now, Hoover Limited will be heading for a further loss in 1981. This business cannot survive if we continue to lose money.

Meetings are taking place throughout the Company today to tell our employees of the crisis we are facing and of the Company's determination to effect a major improvement in the situation. The proposals we are announcing are designed to achieve a return to profitability during this year.

In Merthyr we are proposing a redundancy of around 300 people and a continued programme of short-time working.

In Perivale we are proposing a redundancy of around 200 people and a continued programme of short-time working.

In Cambuslang we are proposing a redundancy of around 400 people and a continued programme of short-time working.

In the Head Office of the Company at Perivale we will be reviewing all jobs during this month with a view to eliminating unnecessary work.

On completion of his general statement on the UK subsidiary, Mr Bristow spoke specifically about Perivale's performance. He said that sales of the factory's products were 'disappointingly low' and that stock levels had not been reduced to the desired level. He added that, unless further corrective action was taken, stock levels would continue to rise.

The following day, Perivale management met the Joint Wages Committee (Combined) to discuss the 'Redundancy and Short-time Working Programme'. Members of the JCC were highly critical of the company's proposals. According to one member, the number of workers involved in the production process had been disproportionately reduced compared with the number in administration. For example, between January 1975 and 1981, the number of manual direct workers had been reduced by 44.5 per cent, from 1283 to 712, whereas the number of manual indirects was cut by only 19 per cent, from 609 to 494. The factory convener criticized Hoover for failing to invest in 'people or plant in order to develop products or plant'.[24]

The following month, on 23 April, Mr Bristow explained to the JCC that short-time working would end, as Perivale had obtained approval to produce 60 000 special hard bags for the Hoover Junior vacuum cleaner. He also revealed that A. T. Kearney, a management consultancy firm, had been recruited to investigate Hoover's UK operations, particularly the floor-care business.[25]

Four months later, on 25 August 1981, Peter Budd, Hoover's associate director in charge of personnel, met the Perivale shop stewards to review 'many of the problems facing our Company's manufacturing operations'. He reminded them of the meeting the previous year at which the company informed employees of its four major problems: falling sales, high stocks, a shortage of cash, and overmanning. He said that redundancies and short-time working had been necessary, for 'without them we may not have been here today; but they did not go far enough'. He stated that the root cause of Hoover's 'profitability problem' was overmanning and increasing wage costs[26].

He told Perivale shop stewards that,[27]

> In general, it is apparent that we must undertake a very positive restructuring of our manufacturing facilities in all three plants. This must involve the rationalization of premises and further manpower reductions ....
>
> It is the production of our UK floorcare range which offers the greatest scope for rationalization and A. T. Kearney have now reported on the options available to us for the Directors to evaluate. These options are:
> 1. Slim down Perivale and Cambuslang to manning and cost levels which bear international comparison.
> 2. Concentrate Floorcare manufacture at Cambuslang and close Perivale.
> 3. Concentrate Floorcare manufacture at Perivale and close Cambuslang.
> 4. Consider alternative sites where Floorcare will be manufactured at the minimum cost to the Company.

Mr Budd stressed that Hoover had not yet decided which option to pursue. He also listed other measures that had been deemed necessary for re-structuring the UK operation. These included new work practices, a longer wage agreement (30 months instead of 12), a reduction in manning levels, no wage increases or industrial action until the company returned to profitability, and the centralization of wage negotiations.

Shop stewards were informed that Hoover's UK subsidiary was making a loss, that sales were down, and that high inflation and the strong pound made it particularly difficult for Hoover to compete with its foreign rivals. Mr Budd described the loss of £6.1 million for the first half of 1981 as 'unacceptable' and stressed that this situation could not continue: 'Let me repeat—this business cannot survive unless we make profits. We must start making profits *now*.'[28] But this would not be easy, particularly as unit sales of the UK subsidiary's products were well down on previous years. For example, in 1977 Hoover PLC's floor-care sales amounted to 1779 units, and laundry equipment sales were just under 700 units; in the first half of 1981 the UK subsidiary made just 581 units of floor-care sales and only 227 units of laundry equipment sales.

The proceedings closed with Mr Budd informing the stewards that he looked forward to meeting them again to discuss their 'considered reply'.

Two days later, shop stewards at Cambuslang called on the company to issue a clear statement on the plant's future, and they agreed to meet their counterparts from Perivale to discuss the common threat of closure.

The Scottish press still believed that Perivale was 'safe' because it was not only Hoover's headquarters, but the only plant owned by the company. It also contended that Merthyr Tydfil was unlikely to be closed as it was Hoover's sole UK source for washing machines, and the company was committed to maintaining this product line.

On 17 September, a meeting organized by the AUEW was held in Brighton of officials from Hoover's three UK plants. A coalition was formed to reply to the company's proposals. It requested from Hoover a copy of the consultants' report which Hoover had commissioned on its UK operations, so that its recommendations could be considered.

On 28 September 1981, at an extraordinary meeting of the JCC at Perivale, Mr Budd assured shop stewards that 'No decision has been made as to the future of this factory.'[29]

On the following day, staff at Perivale met Mr Budd. The meeting appears to have proved unsatisfactory to staff employees, for they wrote to Mr Rawson, chief executive of the US parent, complaining that Mr Budd had given the impression of being 'deliberately provocative in order to prompt an unruly or abusive response to portray the Perivale Management staff in a bad light to justify the plan to close down the Perivale factory'. The letter was sent to the chief executive because staff employees believed that he was about to make 'a decision on the future of the UK manufacturing organization'. The statement was prepared in the hope that it would produce a decision favourable to Perivale.[30]

Another staff statement was issued around this time. It included the following passage:[31]

> The opinion of most of the people we speak to ... is that the Executive have already made up their mind long ago that they will close Perivale, and all this activity, including the engaging of the consultants, is a not very convincing charade in an attempt to give the eventual announcement some credibility. This might be totally untrue, but you should perhaps spend some time considering your past record, your attitudes and your communications with your employees that give rise to these strongly held beliefs, because such a credibility gap is not conducive to creating a strong and profitable Company.
>
> Hence we are not sure if we can take your statement, 'The decision we finally make will be *significantly* influenced by the outcome of the discussions we have in coming weeks', at its face value.

On 16 October, directors of Hoover PLC promised that the period of uncertainty surrounding UK operations would end within a week, by which time the company would have decided which of the four options to follow. An undertaking was given to national officials that the company would make its decision regarding rationalization of manufacturing facilities by 23 October. Mr Goode, managing director of the UK subsidiary, said: 'it would be impossible to deny the possibility of plant closures'.[32]

A week later, on 23 October 1981, Hoover announced its rationalization plans. Cambuslang and Merthyr Tydfil would lose a further 350 and 400 jobs, respectively. These two plants had won a reprieve, but only at the expense of Perivale, which would close with the loss of 1100 jobs. The decision had been taken, it was said, under the direction of parent-company headquarters in Ohio.

With the benefit of hindsight, industrial reporters saw the economic logic in closing Perivale, whereas before the announcement they had argued, by the same criterion, that Cambuslang would be closed. It was now claimed that perhaps the telling factor in the decision to close Perivale was the attraction of raising capital by redeveloping its 9-acre site. In addition, Cambuslang was the most modern plant, and so it made sense to transfer production from Perivale and invest in new production facilities. It was also suggested that Hoover had been under pressure to maintain the Scottish site and avoid a further sharp increase in unemployment in an area notorious, even by Glasgow standards, for its deprivation. Besides, the Cambuslang factory was located in a Special Development Area and was therefore eligible for government grants.

After this announcement, Hoover's UK management met shop stewards on a number of occasions, but they continued to deny shop stewards access to the consultants' report on which the closure decision was based.

Perivale closed in May 1982—seven months after the closure announcement—with the loss of 1100 jobs.

5.5 Conclusions

Foreign divestment theory

The plant closures considered here reflected the fact that all three companies— Singer, Grundig and Hoover—had lost many, if not all, of their ownership-specific advantages. Moreover, compared with Europe, the Far East had stronger location-specific advantages for manufacturers of sewing machines and consumer electronics.

The Singer and Hoover cases confirm the appropriateness of the eclectic theory of foreign divestment which encompasses condition-, motivation- and precipitating-circumstance-based theories. Market conditions had changed substantially since the time of the original investments, and in the case of Singer it is surprising that the Clydebank plant stayed open so long. These changes led to losses, providing the motivation for closure, and the appointment of new men at Singer and Hoover removed any 'barriers to exit'.

In all three cases, there is no question that the foreign divestment decision was made by parent-company executives, although in the Singer and Hoover cases UK management played a key role in implementing the divestment.

Employee disclosure and consultation

The actions of the work-force at Singer Clydebank did little to improve the industrial relations record of Clydeside. From early 1978, it was apparent that the Scottish plant faced closure; but instead of persuading Singer of the value of its Clydebank plant, the workers' actions would suggest that they welcomed closure. Singer gave employees eight months' notice, almost three times the UK's minimum legal requirement.

In contrast, employees at Hoover Perivale were determined to save their jobs. In September 1981, the month before closure was announced, they accused the company of having reached a final decision to close Perivale in the April. Bear in mind that Hoover had told its work-force that four options were under consideration, two of which involved the closure of either Cambuslang or Perivale. As a result of this disclosure, shop stewards at plant level in Scotland and Perivale were claiming the superior performance by their respective plants, and implicitly were arguing for closure of the other. Hoover gave the Perivale work-force seven months' notice, more than double the UK's minimum legal requirement.

While both US multinationals far exceeded the minimum requirement, Grundig gave just 101 days' notice, 11 days more than the legal minimum. This closure, unlike the other two, was totally unexpected.

References

1. M. C. McDermott, *Singer's Clydebank: The Anatomy of Closure*, Undergraduate dissertation, University of Glasgow, 1982.
2. 'Singer's saving stitch in time', *Management Today*, June 1966.
3. Singer, *Singer Shareholder News Letter*, third quarter, 1979.
4. Shop Stewards' Singer Clydebank, press release, 22 March 1978.
5. J. Flavin, Chief Executive Officer, The Singer Company, letter of 22 June 1979 to Clydebank employees.
6. Ibid.
7. Singer Shop Stewards' Factory Committee minute book, factory meeting, 27 June 1978.
8. Ibid.
9. Singer Shop Stewards' Factory Committee minute book, factory meeting, 3 October 1979.
10. Singer Shop Stewards' Factory Committee minute book, factory meeting, 6 October 1978.
11. Singer Shop Stewards', press release, 29 November 1978.
12. 'Singer Saving Scheme', *The Guardian*, 30 November 1978.
13. Singer Company (UK) Ltd, statement of 12 December 1978.
14. 'Productivity demands rejected by Singer workers', *Financial Times*, 14 December 1978.
15. Singer, 'New York, New York, December 13', 13 December 1978.
16. Singer Shop Stewards' Factory Committee minute book, factory meeting, 21 December 1978.
17. Singer Shop Stewards' Factory Committee minute book, factory meeting, 12 January 1979.
18. Interview with former Grundig manager who wishes to remain anonymous.
19. Accounts of Hoover plc.
20. The Hoover Company, *Annual Report*, 1980.

21. 'Hoover set to close Scots plant', *Sunday Standard*, 16 August 1981.
22. Minutes of the 37th Ordinary Meeting of the Joint Consultative Committee, 18 August 1980.
23. Minutes of the 38th Ordinary Meeting of the Joint Consultative Committee, 4 March 1981.
24. Ibid.
25. Minutes of company–union meeting, Perivale, 23 April 1981.
26. Hoover plc, *Manufacturing Review*, 25 August 1981.
27. Ibid.
28. Ibid.
29. Hoover Shop Stewards, minutes of meeting of 28 September 1981.
30. Hoover staff, staff statement to Mr Rawson, chief executive of the Hoover company, 29 September 1981.
31. Hoover staff statement, undated.
32. 'Axe Poised over Hoover plant', *Glasgow Herald*, 17 October 1981.

6
The tyre and rubber products industry

6.1 Introduction

During the 1980s, the tyre industry has undergone significant transformation. During the first half of the decade, some companies were fighting to remain profitable (see Table 6.1), and divestment was the order of the day. In the second half of the 1980s, major tyre companies proved attractive takeover targets. The largest of all, Goodyear, successfully fought off a hostile bid by the Anglo-French financier, Sir James Goldsmith. Others lost their battle to remain internationally competitive and independent. Acquisition or merger has become a key means of expansion in the tyre industry, as in other sectors. The most noteworthy deal (as of December 1988) has been Bridgestone's $2.6 billion acquisition of Firestone, in which Japan's largest tyre producer outbid Italy's Pirelli in the largest ever Japanese acquisition of a US company.[1]

Focus in this chapter is not on acquisition activity of the later 1980s, but on the foreign divestments of the early 1980s and late 1970s, when manufacturers were forced to restructure operations to overcome the unfavourable market conditions that prevailed at that time.

In all, this chapter concentrates on five plant closures: two each by the US MNCs Goodyear and Firestone, and one by the French MNC, Michelin, Europe's largest tyre producer. Executives seeking an insight into the successful implementation of a foreign divestment strategy are directed to the section on Goodyear. This MNC closed a plant at Drumchapel, Scotland, in 1979 and another four years later at Craigavon, Northern Ireland, where

Table 6.1 Net income of Firestone, Goodyear and Michelin, 1979–85 ($ million)

Year	Firestone	Goodyear	Michelin
1985	3	411	110
1984	102	411	(256)
1983	111	306	(286)
1982	6	330	(633)
1981	135	368	67
1980	(106)	312	66
1979	113	202	128

Sources: corporate accounts; *Fortune*

rubber products but not tyres were produced. In both instances, the company's careful attention to detail allowed it to divest with its reputation untarnished. In the Drumchapel case it was the employees themselves who, despite repeated company warnings, precipitated closure.

Trade union officials too should take note of the Goodyear case and of the risks involved in attempting to call the bluff of a large MNC; more recent events involving Ford and British trade unions highlight the disastrous consequences of disregarding corporate warnings (see Chapter 1).

The conduct of Firestone and Michelin in the divestment process was in marked contrast to Goodyear's, and both received strong condemnation from union officials and some politicians for their failure to consult with employees before announcing closure. The French MNC, it should be noted, may have surprised its work-force with the foreign divestment decision, but it did not close its plant as soon as legally permissible: in fact, Michelin considerably exceeded the UK's minimum legal requirement of 90 days' notice.

Firestone's conduct was the more reprehensible, as will be seen, and perhaps this is an indication that firms involved in foreign divestment, and with no other investment in the host country, or plant to invest there in the foreseeable future, are particularly prone to minimize or avoid negotiation and discussion.[2]

Before examining the individual divestments, a review is provided of the world and UK markets for tyres in the late 1970s and early 1980s.

6.2 The tyre market: a review

The tyre industry has traditionally been dominated by US and European MNCs. In the 1960s Goodyear, Michelin and Firestone had expanded their production facilities. Existing plants were extended, new plants opened and growing employment levels set for their worldwide operations. By the late 1970s–early 1980s, these major Western producers were forced to rationalize their operations to take account of the adverse business environment. The optimistic forecasts made in the 1960s had not been realized. Contrary to estimates within the industry, European and North American demand for car and truck tyres (as original equipment and replacement) fell by 38 million units, from 314.7 million in 1979 to 275.8 million in 1982.[3] Consequently, tyre manufacturers faced serious over-capacity.

The source of this problem can be attributed to the huge popularity of radials, which lasted twice as long as cross-ply tyres. The radial tyre, invented by Michelin in 1948, had begun to conquer the global market in the 1970s, and the French MNC had a distinct competitive advantage. As Michelin strengthened its market position, its US rivals recognized the threat and launched a massive capital investment programme to upgrade their plants and convert them to radial production.

Table 6.2   Worldwide employment levels of Firestone, Goodyear and Michelin, 1977–85

Year	Firestone	Goodyear	Michelin
1985	54 700	134 115	n.a.
1984	59 900	133 371	120 000
1983	60 200	128 760	131 000
1982	65 500	131 665	115 000
1981	72 900	138 487	128 000
1980	83 000	144 860	125 000
1979	107 500	154 373	120 000
1978	112 000	154 291	120 000
1977	115 000	153 033	115 000

Source: corporate accounts; Fortune

By the early 1980s, virtually all new cars produced in France, Italy and West Germany, and all but 5 per cent in the UK, were fitted with radials. Japanese car manufacturers showed the same degree of preference, but in the USA radials accounted for just 60 per cent of the new car tyre production.[4]

Compounding the tyre industry's problems, motorists drove their cars a little less each year in the period 1978–82; the main reason for this was undoubtedly the increase in the price of petrol; the universal imposition of speed limits also led to a reduction in sales of replacement tyres.

The combination of more durable tyres, more cost-conscious motorists and changes in driving habits had the expected effect on the tyre industry, and to compound the problem there was a 5 per cent decline in sales of new cars in the largest 'Western markets'—i.e. the USA, Germany, France, Britain and Italy.

At the same time, Toyota, Nissan and Honda had made great advances in Western car markets by increased import penetration— and eventually all of these companies established a car manufacturing presence in North America. By 1983 Japan had become the world's largest automobile manufacturer, and the tyres for all of its vehicles were supplied by Japanese firms. Consequently, Japan's three major tyre makers—Bridgestone, Sumitomo and Yokohama— increased their share of the world market from next to nothing in the early 1970s to 13 per cent by 1982. Their productivity levels were more than double those attained at the older US and UK plants. A high proportion of Japanese plants were equipped from the start for radial tyre production, and they therefore, unlike their US rivals, avoided the expensive transition from cross-ply.

In this increasingly competitive market, tyre producers were often compelled to seek a short-term advantage, either through improved productivity, which generated surplus capacity, or through technological innovations, which rendered their products more durable but in the long-term lowered demand. Whatever alternative was chosen, it precipitated the need for plant closures and job losses (see Table 6.2).

Rationalization was initiated by two US MNCs, Firestone and Goodrich, which closed plants in Switzerland and West Germany, respectively.[5] Other tyre producers were forced to seek a more drastic solution. In early 1979 Uniroyal, the third largest US tyre manufacturer, sold its entire European operation to Continental Gummi-Werke, West Germany's leading producer. Phoenix, Germany's second largest manufacturer, withdrew completely from the tyre market.

Between 1979 and 1982 the decline in the UK market was particularly severe—16 per cent, compared with 12 per cent for the rest of Europe. Moreover, tyre imports to the UK had increased substantially during this period, from 25 per cent of the market in 1980 to almost half (i.e. 46 per cent) of the market in 1984. These imports came mainly from East Germany, Yugoslavia, South Korea, Poland, Portugal and Turkey. Despite an increase in the number of cars on UK roads, a major shake-out in the tyre industry proved necessary, and between 1978 and 1982 employment in the UK tyre industry was more than halved, from about 45 000 to 22 000.

These job losses were accounted for in plant closures. Following the dissolution in 1979 of its trans-border merger with Pirelli of Italy, Dunlop closed plants at Inchinnan (Scotland), Cork (Eire) and Speke (England). Theoretically, these closures cut capacity by a quarter, but productivity gains were so sharp that in 1983 Dunlop could equal 1979 output levels.[6]

In September 1983 Dunlop sold its 40 per cent shareholding in Sumitomo Rubber Industries, and the bulk of its loss-making European tyre operations, to Sumitomo, Japan's second largest tyre producer. (Ironically, Sumitomo was founded as a wholly owned subsidiary of Dunlop in the 1920s.) This deal had been concluded in utmost secrecy, and Britain's Trades Union Congress referred Dunlop to the OECD's UK national contact point, accusing it of breaching the OECD's Guidelines for Multinational Enterprises.

Plants operated by non-UK MNCs did not escape unscathed. In 1981 Firestone terminated UK production, and the following year Michelin announced the closure of its larger plant in Northern Ireland. Against this background we return to Goodyear, which employed two quite different foreign divestment strategies but in both cases withdrew without prejudice to the corporate image. This was due to meticulous corporate planning, as is illustrated below.

6.3 Goodyear

Goodyear was established in 1898 in Akron, Ohio, and opened its first European plant at Wolverhampton, UK, in 1927. Its first major plant on the Continent was not established until 1949, in Luxembourg. In 1957 Goodyear reinforced its UK presence with the opening of a plant at Drumchapel, on the

Table 6.3 Performance data on Goodyear Tyre and Rubber Company (Great Britain) Ltd 1974–84

Year	Sales (£'000)	Net profit before tax (£'000)	No. of employees
1984	244 121	6 006	5 840
1983	231 760	873	6 302
1982	226 089	(13 656)	6 578
1981	216 476	(17 093)	7 626
1980	217 176	(717)	8 662
1979	206 318	(13 392)	8 998
1978	179 752	(21 401)	10 785
1977	187 571	(507)	11 432
1976	159 267	611	10 979
1975	131 715	92	11 212
1974	111 955	3 605	10 942

Source: Extel Statistical Services

outskirts of Glasgow. In 1967 it opened a facility at Craigavon, Ulster, and by 1979 it had a total of five UK plants. Wolverhampton and Drumchapel produced tyres, Barnsley and Dudley retreaded used tyres, Craigavon manufactured other rubber commodities.

In the 1960s further plants were either acquired or established by Goodyear in France, Germany, Italy, Luxembourg and Sweden. Nevertheless, in 1965 almost half of Goodyear's European employment and a third of its European assets were still in the UK.[7]

After the 1974 oil crisis the fortunes of the UK subsidiary deteriorated sharply, and before the end of the decade it was showing heavy losses. A pre-tax loss of £21.4 million in 1978 outweighed the profit of £18 621 made in the seven years between 1970 and 1976 (see Table 6.3).

In 1979 the Drumchapel plant was closed, and four years later the rubber products factory in Northern Ireland was shut down. A number of factors that prompted the decision to close the Drumchapel site proved irrelevant in the Northern Ireland divestment, and vice versa. This divergence in foreign divestment factors appears to have influenced Goodyear's divestment strategy and its employee disclosure and consultation policy. The Drumchapel closure is examined first.

Drumchapel

Background

Beset by excess capacity in the late 1970s, Goodyear had to trim its operations. Drumchapel's productivity and labour relations record was the worst among the Goodyear plants in Europe; it was therefore high on the list of candidates for divestiture.

Early in 1978, local management was already meeting with Scottish members of Parliament, local dignatories and senior trade union officials to acquaint them with the problems at the Scottish plant. Management was having ongoing dialogue with the labour force. In May three senior managers of the UK subsidiary told union representatives that Drumchapel's performance would have to improve significantly or closure could follow. Shortly afterwards, the company arranged a meeting with Drumchapel's local MP, Donald Dewar, currently shadow secretary of state for Scotland.

In September 1978 the chairman of the parent company flew from US headquarters to visit the Scottish factory. He told union officials of the three unions represented at the plant that closure had already been recommended but that he was reluctant to act on this advice. He warned that a prerequisite for retaining the factory was a return from 14- to 15-shift working.

The parent company's chairman had a certain empathy for the Drumchapel plant. He had been chairman of Goodyear (Great Britain) in 1957, and he was particularly anxious that the UK subsidiary management ensure that everyone—employees, the media, the community and the politicians—be made aware of the consequences of rejecting the company's proposals.

Subsidiary management appreciated that the parent company was anxious that Goodyear (Great Britain) adhere to the company's general policy of frankness in employee relations. Management therefore did everything possible to ensure that the Drumchapel work-force was fully aware of the problems facing the company, and that an extra shift was essential in order to lower production costs which at Drumchapel exceeded the retail price.

Employee disclosure and consultation

On 8 December 1978, Goodyear presented union officials with its 'Survival Plan' in a broadsheet entitled *Requirements for Continued Operations: Scotland Plant*. It stipulated that six conditions had to be met to save the plant:[8]

A. Factory returns to 15 shift operations.
B. Plant standards of methods, procedures and *manning* to be competitive with other Goodyear Factories.
C. Maximum Plant coverage with piecework rates fair to both Company and Employee with proper piece accountability.
D. Spirit of Union/Management agreement.
E. Company/Union agreements to be abided by in full to the final conclusion.
F. No outside procedure restrictions or actions to be initiated, such as overtime bans, movement of equipment, etc.

The plant manager told employees that[9]

> We are sure that, given the necessary co-operation, our problems can be resolved with the objective that Goodyear will continue at Garscadden for a long time to come.

Despite clear warnings from the company, however, representatives of the Transport and General Workers' Union (TGWU) rejected the six points of Goodyear's 'Plan for survival' at Garscadden, Drumchapel. On 22 December the plant manager emphasized that the magnitude of the plant's losses could not be allowed to continue. He stressed:[10]

> We therefore, must be sure that everybody is aware that, without some meaningful progress towards the implementation of the Survival Programme in the next several days, it will be necessary for us to proceed with whatever course of action is necessary in the circumstances.

By early 1979, Goodyear anticipated employees rejecting its 'Plan for survival', and was busy weighing up the various factors that would come into play in the event of a closure announcement. An official company document dated 11 January 1979, and entitled *Assumption of Closure: Assumption of Closure Based on Anticipated Refusal of Rubber Workers to Accept Proposals that would make the Plant Financially Viable*, highlighted the various factors to be considered in the face of possible divestment, and pinpointed the perceived opportunities and threats that Goodyear would face in the event of closure. For example, Clydeside's notorious reputation in industrial relations was seen as a major plus for Goodyear; management believed that public opinion would be sympathetic to the company and critical of the Drumchapel work-force for refusing to accept the proposals to save the plant.[11]

On the other hand, the document warned that 1979 was general election year in the UK, and that this could encourage the Labour government to resist the closure—an increase in unemployment might sway some Scottish voters. The report also analysed the various layers in the trade union hierarchy and concluded that shop stewards at plant level tended to be the most politically motivated. The summary of the report was entitled 'Most likely sequence of events once closure intention is announced'. It is reproduced in full below.

Summary
of Goodyear Report:

Most Likely Sequence of Events Once Closure Intention Is Announced.[12]

(1) Unions will want to carry on 'negotiations' with the company to dilute the conditions.
(2) Failure to achieve above will result in the following course of action from the Union:
   (a) acceptance of conditions
   (b) intense industrial activity
   (c) acceptance of closure

   (c) is thought most likely after a period of (b)
(3) Acceptance of closure will bring pressure to improve redundancy terms.
(4) There would be no resistance to pay in lieu of notice (90 days), thus a relatively quick closure instead of 90 day wind down.

On 15 January 1979, national and district officials of the TGWU met with management at the plant for further discussion of the company's six-point programme for survival. After the meeting, a company spokesman commented:[13]

Very little progress, if any, was made at the meeting owing to the refusal of the union representatives to accept items in the programme which will provide for better utilisation of plant. This will give the factory the only opportunity to cut its losses and become competitive, in what is a very competitive market.

The spokesman warned that:[14]

the financial losses currently being sustained at the Drumchapel factory cannot continue. Unless substantial progress is made very quickly, then the company will be forced to find some other solution to ensure its survival in the United Kingdom.

Some three weeks later, the chairman and managing director of Goodyear (Great Britain) warned employees that[15]

A return to a fifteen-shift system is the most important aspect of the survival programme. Without this we cannot make the plant viable. All employees should be fully aware of the gravity of our present situation.

Less than a week after this warning was issued, employees were given the opportunity to accept in full the 'Plan for survival', and so prevent the closure of the factory for the time being. However, 500 of the 700 employees chose to reject the plan, thereby giving Goodyear ample justification for closing Drumchapel. Of this 500, most were still confident that the company was bluffing; others refused on principle to accept the extra Friday night shift, as only a few years earlier a protracted strike, lasting 11 weeks, had achieved the abolition of this shift which had been highly unpopular among the work-force.

The factory convener had been in no doubt that Goodyear would close Drumchapel unless its conditions were met by the workforce:[16]

We put it very strongly to the men that if they did not accept these proposals, however unpalatable they are, then the plant would be closed completely and not only their jobs but those of others in the factory would go. ... The Company have left us in no doubt that it would be closure unless the plan was accepted.

On numerous occasions, the Scottish media have been highly critical of foreign-owned firms closing their Scottish operations, but in this instance it blamed the work-force. One newspaper ran a headline which said it all:[17]

Clydeside tyre workers vote away their jobs

On 20 February, the chairman and managing director of Goodyear's UK subsidiary informed employees, trade unions and the appropriate government departments of the company's decision to close Drumchapel. This was Goodyear International's first ever plant closure. UK management prepared thoroughly for meetings with employees and the media. Recommended answers were prepared.[18]

At last, the Drumchapel work-force accepted that Goodyear had not been bluffing. Another mass meeting was hastily convened for 25 February. Management at Drumchapel relayed news of this development to UK headquarters, warning that employees would now accept the fifteenth shift and adding that, while the Scottish press had been hitherto favourable to the company, its view might change 'when there is no company response to acceptance of the 15th shift by the Union'. It therefore advised that Goodyear should have[19]

> a position which reflects its complete scepticism about the Unions' ability to 'deliver the goods' at the end of the day, particularly in the area of performance on a continuing basis.

The Drumchapel management cited six reasons for scepticism on Goodyear's part, including industrial stoppages, failure to meet production targets and high absenteeism.

As expected, on 25 February the work-force reversed its original decision, and accepted all of Goodyear's conditions. But the divestment decision was final. The plant closed, with the loss of 800 jobs, 89 days after the closure announcement.

Craigavon

Background

Goodyear's Craigavon factory, which was opened in 1967, manufactured conveyor belting, fan belts, rubber hoses and a variety of other industrial rubber products. At its peak in 1976 it employed 1800 workers, but it lost money right from the start, and by the early 1980s employees realized that the plant's future was, at best, uncertain.

In October 1980, 100 employees were put on a three-day week, and by the end of November half the work-force was on short-time. Despite this, local management assured employees that[20]

> there is absolutely no substance whatsoever in the suggestion that Goodyear is pulling out of Northern Ireland. We have every intention of maintaining our presence in Craigavon and look forward to the long term with optimism.

Seven months later, in June 1981, 300 redundancies were announced, and Goodyear predicted that Craigavon would lose £4–5 million in 1981. The plant director gave an assurance that no further redundancies were contemplated, 'and that production of the company's industrial rubber products would continue at Craigavon'.[21]

Reduction in manpower was only one of a series of options tried and tested. They all failed to reverse the tide of increasing losses, and in April 1982 it was revealed that in the previous year Craigavon had suffered its heaviest loss since opening.

Over the next 12 months there was no improvement, and in the first week of March 1983 one of the parent company's vice-presidents, along with senior Craigavon management, met the secretary of state for Northern Ireland to spell out the plant's problems. Ominously, the company statement following these discussions warned that there would be a further performance evaluation of the Ulster plant later in the year, and the situation was described as 'clearly serious'. The fact that Goodyear saw fit to dispatch one of its most senior men from across the Atlantic to Ulster underlined the gravity of the situation.

Two months later, the newly appointed chairman of the US parent decided that Craigavon should be closed. Senior management at the UK subsidiary's Wolverhampton headquarters were informed. They proceeded to prepare a masterplan in which every possible eventuality was carefully considered, and a timetable of events prepared.

The divestment strategy prepared by UK management was outlined in three internal company documents: *Goodyear–Craigavon: Lead-in To Plant Closure, Goodyear–Craigavon: Plant and Technical Centre Closure* and *Goodyear–Craigavon: Closure of Plant and Technical Centre.* These show that Goodyear aimed to achieve the closure of Craigavon 'with an orderly rundown of production/work, with no industrial action, and at minimum cost'. The company was confident that Wolverhampton workers would not resort to industrial action in support of their Ulster colleagues.[22]

Goodyear did expect some reaction from its Craigavon employees, however:[23]

> Employees in the plant believe a major statement will be made shortly.
>
> An announcement in July will not be unexpected but people are anticipating some production to continue but with a very much reduced work-force.
>
> Closure will come as a shock, with dismay, but this is very much the way of life in the Province.
>
> People know how bad the results are—[the Plant Director's] last Presentation was given March 1983. Also, people are aware of the discussions with James Prior, Secretary of State for Northern Ireland held with Ib Thomsen in early March 1983.
>
> People will put up some token resistance to save the plant—the following are possible:
> — Involving National Officials of the Trade Union.
> — Seeking discussions with local MPs as well as those from the European Parliament.
> — Attempting to get public opinion on their side through the *Lurgan Mail* and other newspapers; also the TV.
> — Getting dignatories to make approaches to the Company.
> — Letters to Mercer, Thomsen etc. [i.e. senior parent company executives].
>
> Once the resistance phase is ended and plant closure becomes accepted, people will then turn their minds to getting improved severance payments.

The company also anticipated that the local community would be shocked by the closure decision, as the extent of the factory's problems had not been fully appreciated. The *Lurgan Mail* newspaper was identified as 'the one which could do the Company most harm'.[24]

On 25 June the first step of the divestment strategy, prepared by UK management, was implemented. The parent company chairman, the president of Goodyear International and the chairman and managing director of Goodyear (Great Britain) met the minister of state for Northern Ireland. They told him that Goodyear could no longer continue production at the loss-making Craigavon plant, and employees would be informed of this decision in the near future.

Two days later, the parent company's chairman wrote thanking the minister for meeting him and his two colleagues, 'despite the rather short notice of our visit'. He reminded him that Craigavon's losses since opening exceeded $100 million, 'most of which occurred in the past five years'.[25] The chairman paid high tribute to Craigavon's labour force and their representatives:[26]

> Our dealings with trade unions and our workforce have at all times been both responsible and realistic and have enabled us to make significant gains in productivity which, unfortunately, failed to offset the price erosion in the market.

He added:[27]

> This is a most unpalatable decision for both Goodyear and Northern Ireland and we have agonised deeply over the impact that this decision would have on your Government's effort to reindustrialise Northern Ireland.
>
> However, I would be remiss in my duties to our shareholders if I did not take action in the light of our present projections.
>
> I hope that we can postpone any official announcement until the end of July in order to open negotiations with our employees for an orderly shutdown which should definitely precede any public announcement.

On 29 June, the five most senior executives of Goodyear's UK subsidiary met to review the Craigavon divestment strategy. They knew that Goodyear would be releasing second-quarter results on 2 August, and that these included the write-off costs for closing the Ulster plant. They therefore had to ensure that closure was announced in advance of this date. The proposal to issue notification of closure on 28 July had been approved by the US board, and it was agreed that Craigavon would close on the ninetieth day after the closure announcement, namely on 28 October 1983:[28]

> Pressures to continue production on a reduced basis should be resisted.

A management team of seven was selected for handling the closure. Three of these were based at UK headquarters in Wolverhampton, and the other four were employed at the Craigavon plant. Only the three executives based on the mainland would be involved throughout the divestment process. Top UK executives decided that[29]

> The four Northern Ireland people ... should be informed at a time when it becomes absolutely necessary and no earlier.

All Craigavon's employees began their annual fortnight summer break on 11 July. They were to return to work on Monday 25 July. On Sunday afternoon, 24 July, the personnel manager at Craigavon issued invitations to union officials employed at Craigavon to attend a meeting to be held early the following morning. Some union officials suspected then that the closure of the plant would be announced.

At the same time, the company contacted Tom Murray, a full-time official with the Amalgamated Transport and General Workers Union. He was told that closure would be announced to employees the following day. Goodyear believed that Mr Murray would have 'a major influence' on the employees' reaction to the closure announcement: 'he has handled the Michelin closure— he is one who normally urges restraint'.[30]

Goodyear believed that its announcement would be 'unlikely to trigger any hostile reaction', and took comfort in the knowledge that 'by and large the Craigavon workforce have reacted predictably in the past to situations— they have demonstrated that they do not live "in cloud cuckoo land"'.[31]

On 25 July, employees were told that Craigavon would close on 28 October 1983, with the loss of 756 jobs. They were told that the company's decision was final. The American managing director of Goodyear (Great Britain) said that key divestment factors were the depressed market conditions and the poor performance of the factory. Craigavon had sustained heavy losses since its opening—£8 million in 1981, £6 million in 1982 and, while operating at less than a third capacity in the first seven months of 1983, £4.5 million for that period.

The Craigavon work-force made little attempt to persuade Goodyear to reverse its decision. Even it realized that the Craigavon investment had been ill-advised, and that Goodyear had been slow to concede this fact.

6.4   Firestone

Brentford

Firestone was founded in 1900, and shortly before its thirtieth year established its first manufacturing plant outside of North America. As with so many other US MNCs, it chose the UK as its first European base, and in 1928 it began production at Brentford, near London. Almost 40 years later, it boosted its UK presence with the opening of a plant in Wrexham, Wales. Both these plants were closed within two years of each other in the late 1970s/early 1980s. The general background to the closure decision is presented below, emphasizing in particular Firestone's European operations.

Background

By the mid-1970s, Firestone was multinational in the true sense of the word, having international operations scattered throughout Europe and Latin America.

Between 1970 and 1975 foreign sales doubled, and, according to its *1976 Annual Report*, the company expected this growth rate to be matched in the second half of the decade. This expectation was not realized, and within 12 months it was evident that the projection was off-course. In the *1977 Annual Report*, Firestone's chairman conceded that the company had faced 'unexpected challenges', the European market being the 'major international problem'. He diagnosed over-capacity as a causal factor.

By 1978 these difficulties were reflected on the bottom line. Firestone suffered a loss of $148 million, compared with a profit of $110 million the previous year (see Table 6.1 above). A return to profitability demanded a slimmer overseas operation. Firestone subsidiaries produced tyres and tubes in six European countries: France, Italy, Portugal, Sweden, Switzerland and the UK. The US MNC also had an affiliate in Spain. Within these nations some plants were now surplus to Firestone's requirements, and drastic cuts in plant and labour were required.

The first European plants to close were those situated in Sweden and Switzerland. The handling of these divestments proved controversial. For example, Swiss unions reported Firestone to the Committee for International Investment and Multinational Enterprises for failing to comply with the OECD's Guidelines, and a Swiss court found Firestone guilty of violating a collective agreement, and imposed a fine of SFr 2.6 million. In Sweden, too, the company achieved notoriety: there, 350 employees at its Viskafors plant received only six *weeks'* notification of closure, instead of the six *months* to which they were entitled. The Swedish government intervened, ordering Firestone to guarantee employment for the work-force throughout the period specified by national law.

The International Federation of Chemical, Energy and General Workers (ICEF) Secretariat thus warned affiliated organizations that Firestone was embarking on a restructuring programme, and that it was 'intent upon pursuing this programme in a high-handed, non-cooperative and socially irresponsible manner'.[32]

It was against this background that Brentford and Wrexham were closed. The English plant, by far the larger of the two, was equipped for cross-ply tyres, demand for which had fallen as they were superseded in the mid-1970s by radials. Output was cut back, and this exerted upward pressure on unit costs as economies of scale were lost. The Brentford factory had become a millstone round the company's neck, and was largely responsible for the £6 million loss in 1979 of Firestone's UK subsidiary.

Employee disclosure and consultation

On 14 November 1979, the day after John J. Nevin was elected president of Firestone, the company announced that the 51-year-old Brentford factory would close on 15 February 1980, with the loss of 1500 jobs. At the same time, a statement issued by headquarters in Akron warned that there would be further closures or rationalization in Europe. A gross cost of £33 million was placed on all European closures.[33]

Firestone was criticized for failing to inform and consult with the English work-force. On 14 December, a member of Parliament asked the secretary of state for employment what notification and representations he had received 'concerning Firestone Tyre and Rubber Company's decision to close Brentford'. In his written reply on behalf of the minister, the MP Jim Lester stated that the Department of Employment was notified on 14 November 1979, 'in fulfilment of its obligations under section 100 of the Employment Protection Act 1975'.[34]

Wrexham

Background

Despite the Brentford closure, employees at the Welsh plant expected production there to continue, although it had a history of poor industrial relations and had been dogged by unofficial stoppages: in the first half of 1978, 42 were recorded.

Following this prolonged unrest, the Advisory, Conciliation and Arbitration Service (ACAS) received an invitation in February 1979 from the plant manager and the unions to conduct a survey on industrial relations throughout the Wrexham factory. The ACAS observers reached the following conclusion:[35]

> We see training of management of all levels in industrial relations as one of the foremost needs of the plant at present. Management also needs an awareness of the new circumstances arising from the growth of individual statutory rights and the expansion of employment law in the last few years.

They also found that, in terms of information disclosure, employees were the victims of negligent management and incompetent union representatives:[36]

> We found communication blockages throughout the plant—between different management levels, between departments, between the unions. Management quite complacently considered they had discharged their obligations about passing information by simply telling the union representatives, who often kept it to themselves.

Employee disclosure and consultation

On 23 March 1980, four months after the Brentford closure announcement, management and shop stewards at Wrexham met to discuss short-time working. Some redundancies were issued. A week later a four-day week was introduced. On 18 June further discussions were held on short-time working and redundancy. Firestone was represented by its UK managing director and its UK industrial relations manager.

Two days later, Firestone informed union representatives that 95 employees would be made redundant 'due to a reduction in demand for our products'. On the last day of June, all 600 workers at the Wrexham factory were put on a two-day week, in what the company described as a 'final bid to stave off redundancies'.

Almost six weeks later, and only nine months after its promise of further investment at Wrexham, Firestone announced that it was selling its retail outlets in the UK to Kwik-Fit Holdings for £3.3 million. The company secretary of Firestone's UK subsidiary gave an assurance, however, that production would be maintained at Wrexham.[37]

Union officials were disturbed by the company's proposed sale. Jim Morris, divisional officer of the TGWU, contacted the office of UK managing director, 'requesting an urgent meeting to discuss the overall situation, but specifically the Wrexham factory and Hawarden Distribution centre'.[38]

On 7 August Mr Morris was informed by Mr Tamplin, corporate personnel manager, that, while Mr Fitzpatrick was 'willing to have a meeting', he felt that 'at this stage it would not have a useful purpose because the company in America have not reached any final decision'.[39] This would confirm that the decision to close Wrexham was a centralized one.

Mr Morris, however, was not satisfied by Mr Tamplin's message, and so he wrote as follows to Mr Fitzpatrick:[40]

> In my view we do need an urgent meeting, as we would like to discuss the situation with you prior to any firm decision being taken by the parent company, otherwise all we would be faced with at a future meeting would be a fait accompli one way or the other.

On 19 August, Firestone revealed that, in the first nine months of fiscal year 1980, it had suffered losses of $98 million on sales of $3.62 billion compared with a profit of $78 million on sales of $3.87 billion for the same period in 1979.[41]

The following day, when the trade union delegation attended their pre-arranged meeting at the company's UK headquarters in Brentford, the UK managing director declared that the parent company had decided to close Wrexham, with the loss of 574 jobs. Firestone had thereby decided to withdraw from the UK market. The company explained its decision in a statement to employees:[42]

> Current losses resulting from overcapacity in a declining market, and the cost/price pressures generated by overcapacity, have necessitated the company examining whether continued production at the Wrexham plant should continue. After due consideration of these studies and options which have included short-time work week, limited redundancies, etc., the company has concluded that the Wrexham plant is no longer viable.
>
> It has therefore been concluded that all production will cease at the Wrexham plant on 18th November, 1980.
>
> Union representatives have been told of this conclusion today and consultations will take place with them over the next few days to determine selection for redundancy and how the close-down of production will be achieved. . . .

By 10 October all but 15–20 employees had been paid off, and on 18 November the factory closed completely.

6.5 Michelin

Michelin, like all Western tyre producers, became a victim of intensive competition in a depressed market whose decline is due, in no short measure,

Table 6.4   Performance data on Michelin, 1977–82 (FFr million)

Year	Sales	Net profit	Total employees
1982	34 567	(4165)	115 000
1981	31 337	(290)	128 000
1980	28 178	815	125 000
1979	22 712	598	120 000
1978	19 671	686	120 000
1977	17 439	675	115 000

Source: corporate accounts; editions of *Fortune.*

to technological developments to their product. Within the space of a year, the French company's fortunes were transformed. In 1980 its net income was more than FFr800 million, but in 1981 it suffered a loss of almost FFr300 million (see Table 6.4); in 1982 it reported a staggering loss of more than FFr4 billion. Retrenchment was the order of the day, and plants were closed in Belgium, Italy and the UK.

Michelin has a reputation for secrecy, and this prominent feature of the French company's corporate culture was apparent in the divestment strategy when it announced the closure of Mallusk in 1982.

In the Goodyear and Firestone closures, it was possible to identify signals that closure loomed; not so with Michelin, even with the benefit of hindsight. The section below examines the impact of the recession on the French MNC's UK subsidiary.

Mallusk

Background and employee disclosure and consultation

Michelin opened its first plant in the UK at Stoke-on-Trent in 1927. During the 1960s and early 1970s it opened five other plants in Britain: one in England at Burnley in 1960; two in Northern Ireland, Mallusk (near Belfast) in 1965, and Ballymena in 1969; and two in Scotland, Dundee in 1972 and Aberdeen in 1973. Of these, the Stoke plant was the largest, but Michelin decided that a significant reduction in excess capacity could be achieved by the closure of Mallusk, the second largest facility, and on Monday, 13 December 1982, Michelin's UK executive director told the minister of state for Northern Ireland that the total closure of Mallusk would be announced on Friday.[43]

On Friday morning, the local radio station telephoned the factory convener asking for his reaction to Michelin's decision to close the factory. The factory convener had not heard of any decision of this kind. Stewards believed that the media was merely speculating. As far as they were concerned, the company had convened a meeting for 1.30 pm to present its pay offer or, at worst, to announce some redundancies. Instead, the union delegation received stunning news: Mallusk was to close.

As the stewards left the meeting, which lasted less than 30 minutes, they discovered that employees had been issued with three forms. In the first, Michelin informed employees that up to 4000 jobs would be lost at its UK plants over the next couple of years; more than half of these would come from the closure of Mallusk. In the second, all of the factory's 2000 employees were served their 90 days' redundancy notice, even though the factory would be phased out 'over about one year', and their terms of redundancy were outlined; it was made clear that these would be reduced unless the work-force co-operated in an orderly rundown. The third form called for 600 volunteers for immediate redundancy.

The following Wednesday, Michelin's decision was the subject of a lengthy debate in the Northern Ireland Assembly. The factory was one of the province's major employers, and its closure represented a loss of 2.3 per cent of total employment in the manufacturing sector of the Six Counties. One politician put the proposed closure in perspective, commenting that it was the equivalent of the UK losing 150 000 jobs in one sweep.[44]

During the debate, a local councillor revealed that he had been told in confidence by a local manager in late October that Mallusk was going to close. His informant had 'leaked' the company's plans to him in the hope that he would be able to launch a public campaign to reverse the decision.[45] When the councillor subsequently approached both management and unions, the former denied that there was any proposed closure, while the latter were convinced that this was indeed the case.

The spirit of that debate was best summed up by two speakers. Mr Allister, councillor for North Antrim, condemned the company, saying:[46]

> Michelin, it seems, has come to epitomise all that is worst in the excesses of the handling by multinationals of their workers. These were job losses which were inflicted on the people affected without the least consultation. There was no consultation whatever with unions from management.

Another speaker, Mr Taylor, a member of the European Parliament, argued that Michelin's handling of the closure announcement was further evidence of the need for the legislation which the Vredeling Proposals offered. He compared the four days' notice given to the public authorities with the original Vredeling Proposals' requirement of a minimum of 40 days' notification to employees before the final decision is made. He concluded:[47]

> I think that throughout Western Europe ... the manner in which Michelin have handled this whole decision will go down as one of the most shameful examples of multinationals in operation.

He said, therefore, that he welcomed the Vredeling Proposals, as they would enforce consultation with employees.

Mallusk closed almost two years later, in 1984.

6.6 Conclusions

The tyre industry's problems were so sudden and unexpected that many factories that were opened in the 1960s were outdated by the late 1970s and had to be closed. Goodyear, Michelin and Firestone confronted similar problems, but as the above case study reveals, the conduct of Goodyear was far removed from that of its American and French rivals.

Foreign divestment theory

Despite increasing oil prices since 1973, the number of motorists continues to grow. Average mileage per motorist continues to decrease, however, and low petrol consumption has become a key consideration in choice of car. Fewer journeys in lighter cars make for less demand for replacement tyres.

But the price of petroleum is perhaps not the main reason for the deflated tyre market. Tyre producers themselves have contributed, albeit inadvertently, to the decline. As a purely functional product, the tyre is replaced only when worn. Unlike the motor car, it does not rely on new short-lived fashions to generate sales among image-conscious consumers. Consequently, product differentiation rests on technological advantage, and so developing a value-for-money, longer-lasting tyre is the one and only key to maintaining sales and market share.

Thus, cross-plys have been superseded by radials, which have themselves been subject to life-prolonging technological improvement. The constant battle to produce increasingly wear-resistant tyres has proved a double-edged sword, for, while the sole route to survival, it creates further excess capacity in an industry that is already victim of the 1960s' over-optimistic forecasts.

Adverse conditions in the late 1970s were in marked contrast to those prevalent in the pre-energy crisis years, when producers had brought large modern plants on stream. This hostile business environment partly explains the plant closures reviewed above, and makes the condition-based theory of foreign divestment a particularly sound model in explaining closures in the tyre and rubber industry in general.

The managerial literature stresses parent-company losses as a major motivation for divestment, and both Michelin and Firestone had suffered such major losses when they closed their UK operations. Goodyear remained profitable throughout the recession, but its UK subsidiary was a drain on corporate resources, and poor subsidiary performance is also a key divestment factor.

As the Drumchapel and Craigavon closures illustrate, strong motivating forces existed for the Akron-based MNC to close these two plants. The 22-year-old Scottish site not only had an appalling industrial relations record, but also catered for a rapidly dwindling market segment—cross-ply tyres. Despite its history, the board chairman's 'softspot' for Drumchapel proved a powerful 'barrier to exit' which impacted upon the company's decision to conduct a publicity campaign of the plant's problems.

The Ulster plant's failure to record a single profitable year in its short 15-year life-span suggests that the original decision to establish the unit was ill-founded. The political climate had changed drastically shortly after the plant opened, and in August 1969 there was an eruption which has bedevilled the province ever since. Employee relations were good, however, and there is no evidence to suggest that the plant was adversely affected by sectarianism.

Craigavon was closed simply because of insufficient demand; the factory was a liability. In addition to the condition- and motivation-based theoretical divestment models, the precipitating-circumstance-based theory provides an important explanatory framework for the Craigavon closure; the decision to close was taken by the new chairman of the board only five months after his appointment.

Michelin's decision to reduce sharply UK manufacturing capacity was clearly a response to deteriorating market conditions. Mallusk was the company's second largest UK plant, after the older Stoke site, which doubled as Michelin's UK headquarters. Greater strategic importance and longer managerial commitment no doubt favoured the older plant. At the time of the closure announcement, Michelin was at pains to stress that Mallusk's location did not influence the divestment decision, but the permanent threat of civil unrest could hardly have endeared the Ulster plant to subsidiary and parent-company management.

Divestment of UK operations was just part of a major rationalization programme in which employment levels were slashed at Firestone. Built before the Second World War, Firestone's Brentford operation, like Goodyear's Drumchapel plant, produced cross-ply tyres whose popularity had slumped during the 1970s. Not surprisingly, Brentford with its outdated product range was mainly responsible for the firm's heavy losses in the UK.

The group's other plant at Wrexham was blighted by a different problem— one that had also dogged Goodyear's Scottish factory. The modern Welsh plant had a history of industrial disputes, and the report from ACAS, commissioned less than two years before closure, reflected a dismal picture of managerial incompetence and employee militancy. These factors no doubt contributed to Firestone's decision to dispose of its UK subsidiary and transfer production to the Iberian peninsula.

The five plants examined in this chapter were opened in 1921, 1957, 1965, 1967 and 1968. By the late 1970s and early 1980s, when they closed, the business environment had drastically changed from the halcyon days of the 1960s. Faced with excess capacity, manufacturers were compelled to rationalize. The motivations for closing these plants can be found in one or more of the following divestment factors which rendered them unviable:

outdated production facilities, low productivity, labour problems, poor pre-investment analysis and, most importantly, low demand.

The role of the 'new man' is evident in the Goodyear Craigavon and Firestone Wrexham cases, the divestment decision being taken four and nine months, respectively, after the appointment of a new chairman/chief executive officer. The close relationship between a change in executive personnel and the difficult divestment decision is particularly noticeable in the other Firestone case: Brentford's closure announcement was issued the day after Mr Nevin's elevation to position of president.

Divestment theory puts forward the proposition that the decision to reshuffle senior management increases the likelihood that another quite different decision will be reached: namely, to sell or close down certain operations. But is this really an accurate interpretation of previous divestment situations? It would be foolish to suggest that, within 24 hours of taking office, Mr Nevin had conducted a review of operations, concluded that Brentford should close and then implemented that decision. It is more realistic to view both events—Mr Nevin's promotion and Brentford's closure—as symptoms of an ailing company, its self-diagnosis and pre-scription being major change, essential in restoring the parent company's fortunes.

If this is the case, the value of precipitating-circumstance-based divestment theory becomes questionable, as it appears nothing more than a self-fulfilling prophesy. However, this hypothesis is of predictive value, in that stakeholders with an interest in anticipating divestment have an additional pointer upon which to base their expectations.

Employee disclosure and consultation

The Goodyear Drumchapel closure is unique in that employees were repeatedly warned by the company that the plant would be closed unless they accepted in full the Survival Plan. Whereas employees normally complain of being hampered by lack of information, the Drumchapel work-force decided its own fate and rejected Goodyear's programme. By providing employees with all the facts, and correctly predicting their rash reaction, the US MNC was able to withdraw from Scotland with its reputation intact, while the work-force was lambasted by virtually all sections of the Scottish media. In this respect it was a perfectly executed divestment strategy—success founded upon total frankness with employees, their representatives and the local community.

Local plant management was also totally involved in employee com-munication. Indeed, the plant manager provided an invaluable service to management at Goodyear's Wolverhampton headquarters. He kept a close monitor of the mood in the plant and forewarned UK management of the labour force's most likely response to the company's proposals. Consequently, management was constantly one step ahead of the work-force, which raced headlong like lemmings to disaster.

The closure of the Scottish operation had been therefore sadly predictable. It was closed 89 days after the closure announcement, 90 days including the day of the announcement (but the Department of Employment states categorically that this day should not be included in calculating redundancy notice). The fact that they received the minimum legal notice is hardly surprising in view of Drumchapel employees' apparent lack of interest in safeguarding their own jobs, and one can hardly blame Goodyear for getting out as quickly as possible.

Closure at Craigavon was also anticipated, but there similarities with Drumchapel end. Goodyear handled the divestment process quite differently, but equally effectively. Instead of directly informing the work-force, the company relied on carefully placed leaks which were reported in the local newspaper.

The decision to close the Ulster plant was made in May 1983 by Goodyear's newly appointed chairman of the board, and senior UK subsidiary management were notified shortly after. The Wolverhampton-based executives embarked upon meticulous preparation for implementing the divestment decision. They had to ensure that employees had been notified by 2 August 1983, and they formally decided to keep local Ulster management in the dark for as long as possible.

Management at Craigavon was fed selected snippets of information by senior UK subsidiary management in the knowledge that it would be passed to the local newspaper, the *Lurgan Mail*. Perhaps discovery of the Craigavon mole and fear of premature publicity explains Wolverhampton's reluctance to inform plant management.

Nevertheless, Goodyear's judicial leak policy braced the work-force for closure. This was announced on 25 July 1983, some two months after the divestment decision had been made in the USA by Goodyear's top man. The news could hardly be described as a bombshell. If anything, the surprise was that closure had not been implemented sooner. Craigavon was closed 96 days later, on 28 October 1983. Goodyear thus exceeded by six days the UK's absolute minimum legal notification requirement.

Goodyear's divestment strategy ensured that closure of both its plants was not unexpected. This was not the case in the Firestone closures, even though British trade unions had been warned by their European counterparts that the company was in the process of rationalizing its European operations. Firestone's notoriously cavalier approach to divestment was underscored by the US MNCs' conduct in the Brentford and Wrexham plant closures.

The work-force at the London plant received no indication of closure from Firestone; 93 days later Brentford closed. Nevertheless a government spokesman confirmed in Parliament that Firestone's conduct was in accordance with UK legislation.

However, it is the Wrexham closure that highlights the difficulties faced by employees trying to extract information from subsidiary management of a foreign parent company. In the Goodyear Craigavon closure, it was seen that the divestment decision was made in the USA and then passed on to subsidiary management, who delayed telling plant management until the last minute.

It is difficult to believe that, by early August 1980, Firestone's UK subsidiary management did not know that Wrexham was to be closed, but if it was genuinely unaware of the fact, then the parent company deserves strong condemnation. If it did know of the divestment decision, the UK management was not only unforthcoming, but the principal perpetrators of an elaborate deception against employees and their representatives.

The sale of the company's retail outlets had convinced union leaders that closure was looming, but UK management freely assured the work-force that the future of the Welsh plant was safe, saying that the parent company had not yet reached a final decision. However, rumours of closure were to prove well-founded. Two weeks after issuing these assurances, Firestone announced the closure of Wrexham. The factory was closed 90 days later. Firestone had therefore conformed with the basic minimum legal requirements of the 1975 Employment Protection Act.

Unlike Goodyear and Firestone, Michelin gave employees almost two years' notice. News of the divestment decision was greeted with condemnation by all local politicians—no mean achievement in sectarian Belfast. Their views and bitter denunciation of the firm are recorded above. Michelin incurred the wrath of the work-force and politicians alike because, unlike Goodyear, it had given no indication whatsoever of its intention to close Mallusk before it presented its *'fait accompli'* in December 1982.

At the time of the closure announcement, more than 20 per cent of Ulster's labour force was unemployed. The province was one of Europe's worst economic and social blackspots. Attracting prospective employers to the Six Counties had proved a major challenge to Westminster, and in desperation the UK government had rashly invested millions of pounds of taxpayers' money in highly suspect projects, notably the DeLorean car and Lear Fan jet.

Tempers were fuelled by Michelin's apparent insensitivity. First, it had notified the public authorities of the impending 2000 job losses only four days before notifying the work-force. Ulster politicians were enraged that such short notice before the public closure announcement denied them the opportunity to hold discussions with the company. This was in contrast to Goodyear, which intimated its intentions to the public authorities a full month before informing employees.

Second, Michelin chose to make the announcement just before Christmas, when it would have had nothing to lose by delaying the news until after the festive season—especially as it was planning a gradual rundown over 12 months. By contrast, seven months later, when Goodyear decided to close

Craigavon, it decided to break the news to the work-force *after* their summer break rather than before, so as to avoid ruining employees' holidays with such a depressing announcement.

Given Michelin's conduct, the statement below rings hollow:[48]

> The directors recognise the importance of good communications and relations with employees. An integral part of such policy is the maintenance and development of two-way communications and encouragement to the employees to identify themselves with the Company.

Of the three MNCs examined in this chapter, Goodyear alone ensured that employees were not taken by surprise at the closure decisions; indeed, the Drumchapel work-force itself effectively took the decision. The conduct of this US MNC therefore stands above that of the Firestone and the French MNC. Nevertheless, the company's own standards, not the OECD's Guidelines, determined Goodyear's behaviour.

A number of points emerge from this chapter. First, the actual divestment decision is always centralized. In one case it was found that, while subsidiary management knew of closure plans, it chose to withhold this information from local management who were the unions' source of information. However, the response of Firestone's UK management to approaches from union officials representing the Wrexham plant suggests that parent-company executives had withheld information from the UK executives, or that the latter had been less than open with employees' representatives.

Second, as for employee disclosure and consultation by Firestone, the former was minimal and the latter non-existent. Michelin gave 18 months' notice, but presented public authorities and work-force with an unexpected *fait accompli*. Goodyear, on the other hand, gave Ulster's civic leaders four weeks' notice, and had indirectly indicated that Craigavon's future was in jeopardy. The Drumchapel case is unique among the closures examined in this book, in that employees, given the choice between employment and redundancy, voted for the latter. A subsequent change of heart served only to highlight the irresponsible nature of the work-force. Goodyear closed Drumchapel as soon as legally possible. It was rid of its worst plant in Europe.

There can be no greater indictment of current UK employment protection legislation than the sad fact of the UK government's statement that Firestone had fulfilled its legal obligations.

References

1. M. C. McDermott and S. J. Gray, 'International mergers: the pursuit of global market leadership'. 15th Annual Conference, European Association for Research in Industrial Economics, Rotterdam, 31 August–2 September 1988.
2. Business International (in collaboration with J. J. Boddewyn), *International Divestment: A Survey of Corporate Experience*, New York, 1976.

3. M. C. McDermott, *Foreign Divestment and Employee Disclosure and Consultation in the UK, 1978–85*, Doctoral thesis, University of Glasgow, 1986.
4. Ibid.
5. N. Hood and S. Young, *Multinationals in Retreat: The Scottish Experience*, Edinburgh University Press, 1982.
6. *The Times*, 20 September 1983.
7. Hood and Young, op. cit.
8. Goodyear, *Requirements for Continued Operations: Scotland Plant*, 8 December 1978.
9. Goodyear, letter of 8 December 1978 from the Drumchapel plant manager to employees.
10. Goodyear, letter of 22 December 1978 from the Drumchapel plant manager to employees.
11. Goodyear, *Assumption of Closure: Assumption of Closure Based on Anticipated Refusal of Rubber Workers to Accept Proposals that would make the Plant Financially Viable*, 1979.
12. Ibid.
13. Goodyear, 'News from Goodyear', statement issued 16 January 1979.
14. Ibid.
15. Goodyear, letter of 8 February 1979 from the chairman and managing director of Goodyear (Great Britain) to Drumchapel employees.
16. 'Clydeside tyre workers vote away their jobs', *The Scotsman*, 14 February 1979.
17. Ibid.
18. Goodyear, 'Questions which may be asked by employees or at the press conference on February 20th 1979', undated.
19. Goodyear, internal memorandum from Drumchapel management to UK subsidiary management, 22 February 1979.
20. '20 jobs lose as Goodyear goes on a short week', *Lurgan Mail*, 21 November 1980.
21. 'No more Craigavon jobs to go', *Belfast Telegraph*, 11 June 1981.
22. Goodyear, *Goodyear–Craigavon: Plant and Technical Centre Closure*, 1983.
23. Ibid.
24. Ibid.
25. Goodyear, letter of 27 June 1983 from the chairman to minister of state for Northern Ireland.
26. Ibid.
27. Ibid.
28. Goodyear (Great Britain), Minutes of meeting of senior UK subsidiary management, 29 June 1983.
29. Ibid.
30. Goodyear, *Goodyear–Craigavon: Lead-in To Plant Closure*, 1983.
31. Ibid.
32. International Federation of Chemical, Energy and General Workers' Union Secretariat.
33. 'Firestone to shut down Brentford plants next year', *Guardian*, 15 November 1979.
34. *Hansard*, 796, 14 December 1979.
35. Advisory, Conciliation and Arbitration Service, *Firestone Ltd*, London, 1979.
36. Ibid.
37. 'Union gives ultimatum to Firestone', *Evening Leader*, 11 August 1980.
38. Letter of 7 August 1980 from J. Morris, divisional officer of the Transport and General Workers Union, to J. Fitzpatrick, managing director of Firestone's UK subsidiary.

39. Ibid.
40. Ibid.
41. 'Firestone to close last UK factory', *Financial Times*, 21 August 1986.
42. Firestone, *Announcement to Sales and Administrative Employees Located at Brentford: Closure of Wrexham Plant*, 20 August 1980.
43. Northern Ireland Assembly, *Official Report of Debates*, 22 December 1982.
44. Ibid.
45. Author's telephone interview with Councillor Agnew, September 1984.
46. Northern Ireland Assembly, op. cit.
47. Ibid.
48. Michelin plc, *Annual Report*, 1984.

7
The agricultural and earth-moving equipment industry

7.1 Introduction

The three MNCs studied in this chapter—Caterpillar, International Harvester (now known as Navistar International) and Massey-Ferguson (now called Varity Corporation)—supply capital goods in markets that are highly unstable, subject to cyclical and seasonal fluctuations.

These three North American corporations have all faced a hostile external environment in recent years, albeit at different times. One crucial factor differentiates Caterpillar from the other two: the internal strengths of the corporation ensured that it escaped the near bankruptcy suffered by the others. Nevertheless, Caterpillar too has come through a difficult period which it could not have expected.

Despite its undoubted managerial skills—hence its position of global market leader in earth-moving equipment—Caterpillar has won notoriety in Britain, if not in Europe, for its approach to plant closures. Since 1984 it has shut down two of its three UK plants, with both closures proving highly controversial, though for quite different reasons.

The Birtley closure announcement aroused interest in the European Parliament because Caterpillar had been a vociferous opponent of the Vredeling Proposals on employee disclosure and consultation, and had written to several MEPs urging that they vote against them:[1]

> We believe that companies should inform and involve employees in matters of concern to them. We make a substantial effort to do so, both within our plants and on a total company basis.
>
> There have been instances in which some multinational companies have failed to communicate adequately on matters of concern to employees, but the vast majority of multinational companies should not be judged or penalised for the shortcomings of a few.

In response to the Birtley closure announcement, the TUC demanded an investigation into Caterpillar's apparent breaches of the OECD's Guidelines for Multinational Enterprises. The assistant general secretary of the TUC stressed that[2]

> Given the current debate on workers' rights in the context of the Vredeling proposals, we must continue to ensure that this is a test case concerning the limits to voluntary guidelines.

As of the end of 1988, Caterpillar remains the only foreign-owned firm which the TUC has referred to the OECD for failing to adhere to its Guidelines during the foreign divestment process.

The Uddingston closure announcement was met with severe condemnation by politicians in Scotland, including the secretary of state for Scotland, who only weeks earlier, in his New Year message, had praised Caterpillar for its commitment to Scotland. In September 1987 Caterpillar had designated Uddingston an important role in its 'Plant With A Future' programme, promising that more than £62 million would be invested in Uddingston; but within 16 weeks, the US parent had decided to close the Scottish facility.

The closures of Birtley and Uddingston are examined below. It will be shown that Caterpillar's reputation in the UK has been badly bruised by its implementation of the divestment strategy. It is difficult to believe that any company could so harm its own image; and other firms planning divestment can find in Caterpillar a model of how *not* to manage the foreign divestment process.

The two cases also highlight the inability of trade unions to reverse corporate decision-making. The Newcastle work-force had recourse to the OECD's Guidelines and the European Parliament, while their Glasgow counterparts staged a lengthy sit-in. From a public relations perspective, both exercises were arguably successful, but in the long-run they proved futile.

In contrast to Caterpillar, Massey-Ferguson and Harvester skilfully prepared their divestment strategies, and paid careful attention to employee welfare. Massey, the Canadian MNC, was especially forthright with its employees. Harvester delayed informing its work-force for some months after the divestment decision had been taken. This latter case is useful in that it reveals the disclosure process within the corporation itself, as much as that pertaining to employees.

7.2   A review of the market

In the late 1970s–early 1980s, Massey-Ferguson, Harvester and Caterpillar all achieved record profits. However, within 12 months of their respective successes, the three North American MNCs found themselves facing heavy losses as strongly unfavourable economic factors impacted on their major markets.

After the mid-1970s, sales of agricultural equipment fell dramatically. Bumper harvests depressed grain prices and therefore farmers' incomes, so (1) they had less incentive to grow grain, and (2) they had a shortage of funds at a time of high interest rates. Replacement buying therefore predominated over new purchases among farmers. This external problem was compounded by the structural weaknesses of Massey and Harvester.

In some respects, Massey was fortunate in that it was the first firm in this sector to fall victim of the depression; therefore it responded earlier than its rivals. By 1981, the world tractor market was at its lowest level since 1945. The industry was operating at only half its capacity, imposing tremendous pressure on production costs. In an attempt to reduce costs, Harvester entered into an expensive five-month labour dispute to win concessions from the United Auto Workers (UAW) union. It borrowed heavily during the strike, and to make matters worse, US interest rates reached unprecedented peaks as the Federal Reserve strived to tame inflation. This fiscal policy compounded Harvester's problems, because farmers, whose incomes had slumped even further owing to the US embargo on grain exports to Russia, could no longer afford to borrow. Between 1980 and 1985, Harvester lost more than $3 billion, and the labour force was slashed from 87 000 to 17 000. Several plants in the UK were closed, but this case focuses on the Bradford plant closure.

Caterpillar's difficulties emerged in 1982. The company was confronted with an array of problems which surfaced simultaneously: worldwide recession; decline in large construction projects as Third World countries' debt problems precluded further developments in their infrastructure; record high interest rates; stronger international competition, mainly from Komatsu of Japan; political exclusion from large markets; a strong US dollar making US exports more expensive; and a seven-month labour strike by the UAW at its North American plants. The company had never experienced problems of this magnitude: 'So many difficulties at one time was unprecedented'.[3]

The dramatic decline in demand for capital goods in the early 1980s was not foreseen. The universal failure of companies to detect the market slump underlines the extent to which firms were caught unaware. Caterpillar was faced with 70 per cent excess capacity by 1982/83 and no indication of a sudden increase in demand for its products.[4]

After suffering losses of almost $1 billion between 1982 and 1984, Caterpillar reported a profit of $198 million in 1985 on sales of $6.8 billion. In 1986 sales rose to $7.3 billion but net income slipped to $76 million. Recovery was incomplete, but employees at Caterpillar's Uddingston plant had grounds for optimism. Yet within 16 weeks of announcing a £62.5 million investment programme, Caterpillar had announced its decision to close the Scottish plant. This was truly a dramatic turnaround, which I shall seek to explain below.

We begin with a review of the Massey-Ferguson Kilmarnock closure. The Canadian MNC, confronted with a recession particularly in the key markets of South America and Turkey, as well as with market saturation in Europe, embarked on a reappraisal of European combine harvester production. This industry case study begins with an examination the corporation's response to these conditions, and considers the review's implications for the Scottish plant at Kilmarnock and its 1500-strong work-force.

Table 7.1 Performance data on Massey-Ferguson, 1977–80

Year	Sales ($m)	Net profit ($m)	No. employed
1980	3132	(225)	41 690
1979	2973	37	56 233
1978	2631	(268)	57 983
1977	2861	3	67 151

Source: corporate accounts

7.3 Massey-Ferguson

Massey-Ferguson was formed in 1953, when Massey-Harris, the combine harvester manufacturer, acquired the Ferguson Company, which had achieved worldwide success in tractors. Five years later, the name Massey-Ferguson was adopted.

Prior to 1977, Massey-Ferguson was controlled by Argus Corporation, a Canadian financial holding company which in turn was controlled by another Canadian holding company, Ravelston. In 1977 Massey reported a net profit of $3 million on sales of $2861 million, but it then entered a period in which it suffered dramatic losses. By 1980 its very survival was in question. Eventually, it was bailed out by some 200 lenders, mostly banks.

Unlike most US MNCs, Massey's domestic market had been of minor strategic importance compared with its foreign operations. In 1977 foreign sales (i.e. sales outside North America) accounted for 70 per cent, while sales in Canada accounted for only 7 per cent of total group sales. Massey therefore could not fall back on a large domestic market in periods of recession. Further indication of the minor role of its home base was the number employed by Massey in Canada: only one-third the number employed in the UK.

By 1977 the slump in demand for agricultural equipment, combined with internal weaknesses, had taken their toll on Massey's share price. By the end of 1977, Massey shares on the Toronto stock exchange had fallen below their 1976 high of $32 back to the 1971 level of $13. Massey was in a vulnerable position. Managerial and financial resources had been fully stretched by its vigorous growth policy, financed by heavy borrowing from the banks. By mid-1978, Massey's borrowings had reached $1.3 billion. In the first quarter of 1978 fiscal year the corporation's losses were running at $8 million for the year, but by the end of the fourth quarter they had risen to $268 million (see Table 7.1). Massey had a severe shortage of funds and a dangerously high debt ratio. Borrowings were almost double equities.

Against this background, in August of that year, the Canadian tycoon Conrad Black gained control of Massey-Ferguson, via Ravelston Corporation, and within a month a new president, Victor Rice, was appointed. Within a year Rice had returned the company to profitability; but then there followed a deeper worldwide slump in the demand for farm equipment. Massey dealers were unable to sell existing stock, let alone place further orders. The company was compelled to borrow further in order to pay interest on previous loans! In order to restore investors' confidence, Rice initiated a four-pronged strategy: (1) reduce inventories through short-time working; (2) divest peripheral businesses; (3) trim the labour force; and (4) rationalize production facilities. This strategy was to have far-reaching implications for the company's Kilmarnock plant.

Kilmarnock

Background

Opened in 1949, the Kilmarnock plant in Scotland originally had a wide product range; but specialization at plant level was introduced in the 1960s, and after this Kilmarnock manufactured medium-sized combine harvesters only. At its peak in the 1960s it employed over 2000 people, and in 1978 the labour force was still 1600 strong. In late 1977 Massey announced a £2 million investment programme, but the dramatic slump in demand that then occurred had been quite unforeseen. Retrenchment rather than expansion was now necessary.

There were seven manual and four staff unions at Kilmarnock, but from September 1978 employees were represented by the Co-ordinating Committee, which was founded in response to workers' perception that uncertainty surrounded the future of the plant.

Employee disclosure and consultation

On 8 September 1978, Massey announced that it was undertaking a Feasibility Study into the rationalization of combine harvester production in Europe, where it had dual sourcing—Kilmarnock, and Marquette, in France. Those conducting the study were given the following 'Terms of Reference':[5]

(1) To evaluate the two single sourcing alternatives available to Massey-Ferguson.
(2) To evaluate the possible alternative uses of the Kilmarnock factory in the event that Marquette is chosen as the single source.
(3) To evaluate the potential expansion of other production currently performed at Marquette in the event that Kilmarnock is chosen as the single source.

Kilmarnock shop stewards believed that the study was a charade, in that a decision had already been taken to close their plant. Their suspicions deepened when they were denied any participation in the exercise, and also by the fact that the report was completed within just five weeks.

The Feasibility Study was published on 27 October 1978, and on 7 November the recommendations of the European Combine Study Group were disclosed for discussion and consultation with the Co-ordinating Committee. The study, not unexpectedly, concluded that Massey had an excess capacity problem in Europe, and that Marquette should become the sole source of European combine harvester production. According to Massey's former director of communications for Europe, Marquette was preferred to Kilmarnock because it was a multi-product operation, and therefore 'the overheads of combine manufacture could be offset into the general overhead at the plant to a considerable extent'.[6] Moreover, as a supplier of parts to other Massey plants in Europe, Marquette was a closely integrated unit, while Kilmarnock was on the periphery not only geographically, but also in terms of Massey's European production strategy.

It was announced that the Scottish plant was not to be closed, however. It would instead produce balers, which had previously been manufactured at Marquette. The employment implications were significant, with 1000 jobs being lost, leaving a depleted work-force of just 500. Massey stated that it would have been cheaper to close Kilmarnock, and that the decision to transfer baler production had been prompted by its 'social responsibility to the area'.[7] Some weeks later, Massey's director of UK operations assured local politicians that this move was not the first stage of its divestment strategy to close Kilmarnock, which would now serve as Massey's sole European source of balers.

Nevertheless, employees remained concerned, and on 2 February 1979 the Co-ordinating Committee met local management to convey its dissatisfaction with the findings of the Feasibility Study. Three months later, on 16 May, management confirmed that 'at this point in time the Study Group did not consider it would be justified in changing its original recommendation'.[8] The Co-ordinating Committee was told that, while no firm decision had yet been made, the planned timetable was to cease combine production on 30 April and commence full baler production on 1 September. Management indicated that a firm decision on the Study Group's recommendations would be made on the week beginning 25 July. It also agreed to the Co-ordinating Committee's request that it be allowed to meet parent company president, Mr Rice, before he made a final decision.

On 4 July Mr Rice met national union leaders in London, and he assured them that he had not yet come to a final decision. Almost a fortnight later, the company announced that the Feasibility Study was to be reopened, and that the deadline for announcing the final decision was being extended. On 23 July, it announced that the study would be updated before any decision on the future of its Kilmarnock plant could be made.

On 9 October Kilmarnock's factory director, Mr Thomas, informed the Co-ordinating Committee that short-time working would be introduced in the week beginning 22 October, and that 950 employees would be on a four-day week. It was also decided that the night shift manning level should be cut by 20 per cent.[9] Exactly a week later, employees were informed that the decision on short-time working would be suspended until Mr Rice decided Kilmarnock's future.

In late October, it was announced from the company's UK headquarters at Coventry that a statement would be issued on 9 November. While the company statement impressed that 'we can give no indication of what this [announcement] may be', it said that it would communicate Mr Rice's decision on Kilmarnock's future.[10]

On 9 November 1979, two days before the plant was due to celebrate the thirtieth anniversary of its official opening, Massey announced that Kilmarnock was to close 96 days later, on 15 February 1980, with the loss of 1500 jobs. It stated that the latest study, initiated in July, revealed that the transfer of baler manufacture to Kilmarnock was no longer viable because of the slump in European sales. It therefore withdrew its offer of baler production and announced the total closure of the Kilmarnock plant, but added that it would continue to undertake the search for other employers, and that Inbucon, a firm of management consultants, was conducting enquiries on the firm's behalf.[11]

The decision to close Kilmarnock was taken only after subsidiary and parent-company management had carefully considered the past results and potential of both sites. Marquette was retained because it had three major advantages over the Scottish factory: it had a foundry on-site; it was located nearer the market; and it was virtually a non-union plant. The former communications director for Europe explained that Kilmarnock was closed because 'The company was losing money in general and on combines in particular. All our competitors in Europe operated from one plant, we had two.'[12]

According to W. Woods, a former shop steward, the final decision to cease all production had been taken at least as far back as September 1978. All discussions held after that, he claims, were a complete waste of time from the union's viewpoint. On the other hand, they met the company's objective, which was to keep hopes alive and at the same time kill off any possibility of organized resistance. Woods argues that this alleged strategy, which was brilliantly executed, achieved Massey's dual objectives: a smooth rundown (not one day's production was lost owing to industrial action), and the enhancement, or at least protection, of Massey's reputation.[13]

Woods believes that the proposed transfer of baler production from Marquette to Kilmarnock, plus the recruitment of Inbucon, were key instruments in the Machiavellian plot carefully designed by Massey. In order to appreciate his argument, an examination of the age structure of the 1500 labour force is necessary. The work-force was composed of three age groups, all roughly equal in size: the over-55s, those between 30 and 55, and those under 30.[14]

According to Woods, Massey's proposal to cease combine production but retain a work-force of 500 for baler production split the work-force and precluded effective industrial action. This proposal was very attractive to all employees except the under-30s. The over-55s were offered very generous redundancy terms, while the middle group were content because they were safe in the knowledge that compulsory redundancies would be based on a last-in-first-out policy. It was therefore only the under-30 group that stood to lose, for, given the brevity of their employment, their severance payments would amount to little, and finding alternative employment in Ayrshire in 1979 would be no mean feat.[15]

The recruitment of Inbucon should be seen, Woods argues, as part of a carefully orchestrated strategy to emasculate the power of labour. As long as employees believed that a buyer might be found for the plant, they were unwilling to support the more militant stewards who were calling for industrial action.[16]

Woods believes that Massey's handling of the rundown of Kilmarnock was a classic case of divide-and-conquer. He argues that the employee disclosure and consultation practised by Massey should not be compared favourably with those firms that gave no advance warning that closure was an option being considered; that the only difference is one of strategy.[17]

Nor were his criticisms restricted to management. He recounted how disappointed he had been with the AUEW's leadership. The Co-ordinating Committee was apparently unwilling to keep other shop stewards abreast of developments at company–union meetings.[18]

As to Vredeling, Woods believes that, while it would be an improvement on UK legislation, it assumes that employees' representatives will pass on information to employees. However, some shop stewards, he alleges, 'often withhold information', and often workers are suspicious of their own stewards.[19]

When Massey-Ferguson revealed its intentions to conduct a Feasibility Study on European combine production, the Co-ordinating Committee at Kilmarnock enlisted the help of several academics, who were to conclude that the feasibility study was 'a post hoc justification of a decision taken for financial (and chiefly cosmetic) reasons. It was primarily a propaganda exercise to undermine damaging labour and government resistance.'[20]

Both the former director of communications Europe and the former Kilmarnock plant manager described the above allegations of Woods and the academics as 'ridiculous'. First, had Massey been concerned only with its public image, a firm less expensive and less professional than Inbucon would have been engaged: Inbucon's services cost Massey £100 000. Second, it did not require a lengthy rundown of the plant, because the machinery was not needed elsewhere; indeed, Massey was prepared to 'give away' capital equipment to any potential buyer. The firm refutes the suggestion that the decision to close had been taken back in 1977 when the review of European combine production was announced. It believes that the majority of former employees at Kilmarnock recognized the company's efforts to minimize the adverse effects on employees as genuine.[21]

The former communications director admits that, if employee disclosure and consultation procedure during the rundown of the plant was in accordance with the Guidelines, then it was by good fortune, not design. Apparent adherence to the Guidelines was, as he admits, purely coincidental.[22]

In 1985, Marquette was closed with the loss of 1150 jobs.

7.4 International Harvester

Formed in 1902 through the merger of McCormick Harvester Company and four other US farm equipment manufacturers, Harvester established its first foreign plants before the First World War, but it was not until 1922 that a UK plant was opened, at Liverpool. In 1946 another UK plant was established in Doncaster. The company's sales reached $1 billion in 1951 and $2 billion in 1964. Between 1964 and 1979 sales grew steadily; in 1979 the company reported all-time record sales of $7.0 billion. Despite this trend, profits were erratic. In 1965 Harvester reported a profit of $109.7 million, but in 1975, after the very high inflation levels caused by the oil crisis, it returned profits of $80.1 million. The company attributed this inconsistency to 'an excessive cost structure' which prevented it from generating enough cash to reinvest adequately in plant and equipment.[23]

Nevertheless, in 1979 Harvester enjoyed record sales and profits of $7 billion and $427 million, respectively (see Table 7.2). This success was due to 'strong market demand, improved market shares, and cost controls'.[24] The company noted with concern, however, that net income as a percentage of net sales was 5.1 per cent, while its major rivals achieved almost double that profit ratio. It blamed this disparity on labour contract provisions, which were more liberal than those of its main rivals. It wanted, therefore, to revise the contract, and this led to a strike at its North American plants which lasted from November 1979 to April 1980. Harvester estimated in May 1980 that the strike had cost the company $225 million.[25]

The return to work at the North American plants did not solve the company's problems, however. In April 1980, US interest rates stood at 20

Table 7.2 Performance data on International Harvester

Year	Sales ($m)	Net income ($m)	No. of employees
1982	4292	(1738)	43 290
1981	6298	(351)	65 640
1980	5208	(297)	87 162
1979	7035	427	97 660
1978	6664	187	95 450
1977	5975	203	96 890

Source: corporate accounts; *Fortune*

per cent. Harvester suffered a loss of $297 million that year. Another major problem was the lowering of Harvester's credit ratings. As a result, the company was excluded from a traditional source of low-cost working capital—the commercial paper market—and instead had to rely on high-cost bank loans. Total company borrowings almost doubled within a year, from $1.4 billion in October 1979 to $2.2 billion the following year. In 1981 numerous businesses were divested, a loss of $394 million was returned, and 1981 was described as 'one of the most difficult years in Harvester history'.[26] The corporation had a worldwide excess capacity problem, and its structural weaknesses had become apparent. America's leading manufacturer of heavy- and medium-duty trucks, and the second largest agricultural equipment manufacturer, had outdated plants, and market and sales were shrinking.[27]

Given the company's external and internal difficulties, foreign divestment was very likely, according to the literature on the subject. The same literature suggests that divestment becomes even more likely when there is a change of top management at the parent-company's headquarters. In the course of 1982 alone, Harvester had three chief executive officers.

By 1982 Harvester was committed to rationalizing its production facilities. Among the UK plants closed was Bradford, which belonged to the Agricultural Equipment division. This closure is reviewed below.

Bradford

Background

Harvester acquired the Bradford factory from Jowett cars in October 1954. The plant produced tractors as well as a range of components for Harvester tractors manufactured at Doncaster, Turkey and India. By 1962 it employed 2250, and exported over 60 per cent of its production. In early 1978 Bradford still employed 1700, but by May the number had been reduced to 1400 in response to falling exports, especially to Turkey, which had grave economic problems.

By 1980 the world market for tractors had fallen drastically, forcing Harvester to conduct a serious analysis of the entire company. Tractor production at Doncaster and Bradford was to be cut by 2000 and 400 units, respectively. As a direct result, short-time working was introduced at both plants. Bradford went on a four-and-a-half-day working week.[28]

Throughout 1981, tractor production was cut back at Doncaster, and therefore at Bradford, which supplied the components. Eventually Bradford ceased manufacturing tractors completely, and merely produced components for assembly operation in Turkey and India.[29]

Employee disclosure and consultation

UK management constantly informed employees' representatives of the 'tremendous problems' facing the parent company and the UK subsidiary

Table 7.3   Performance data on International Harvester of Great Britain

Year	Sales £m	Profits Pre-tax (£m)	Post-tax	Ave. no. of employees
1982	106	(14.0)	(14.2)	3259
1981	119	(18.0)	(18.9)	4629
1980	168	(20.2)	(12.3)	6162
1979	176	2.4	3.3	6653

Source: Extel Statistical Services

(see Tables 7.2 and 7.3), which in 1980 had a pre-tax loss of £20.2 million, with the Agriculture Group alone reporting a pre-tax loss of £9.8 million. Indeed, when Harvester's then president visited Bradford in 1980, according to the plant's former industrial relations manager, he asked what was the cheapest way of closing the Yorkshire site.

On 5 November 1980, union representatives met top UK management to discuss 'job security'. They were told that a 'task force' had been formed to 'review the strategy for Bradford'. They were also told that the UK subsidiary's poor results were due partly to rising costs: in 1977 manufacturing costs were 83 per cent of sales revenue, but by 1980 the former actually exceeded the latter.[30]

On 27 February 1981, management presented shop stewards with a detailed review of the world market for the agricultural equipment industry and its impact on Harvester and its UK subsidiary. It explained that the tractor market was at its lowest since 1945.

Two weeks later, the managing director of Harvester's UK subsidiary told shop stewards that the company was not in the process of formulating a strategy for running down UK operations, leading to total withdrawal.[31] Details of the company's strategy were presented to all employees on a video entitled 'Shaping the Future'. Less than a year later, however, the decision to close Bradford had been taken by the US parent.

On 25 June 1981, management countermanded increasing speculation over the future of Harvester's UK operations:[32]

Faced with these many serious problems it is understandable that there has been much speculation and rumour concerning the future of the British Company. Recent rumours suggested that there would no longer be a manufacturing operation in the UK. Such rumour is without foundation . . ..

In January 1982, 141 redundancies were announced at what the local newspaper described as the 'struggling' Bradford plant.[33] By February the decision to close the Yorkshire plant had already been taken, and UK subsidiary management was busy preparing for closure. The Bradford work-force, however, was not informed of this fact until July, five months later!

Perhaps, significantly, February also saw the unexpected resignation of the British chairman of Harvester's UK subsidiary, just months after taking office. He was replaced by a US executive.[34]

On 11 March, a local newspaper reported that Bradford would close 'unless other work can be found which fits in with the company's worldwide rationalisation plans'. Bradford's industrial relations manager refuted this:[35]

> We are a long way from the position where the closure of the Bradford plant is one of the alternatives being considered.
> We certainly do not foresee further redundancies in Bradford.

This view seemed to be supported by the return in July to full-time working at the Bradford plant, for the first time in two years.

However, unknown to employees and Bradford plant management, since February at the latest, senior UK management had been actively involved in preparing Bradford's closure. An internal company document entitled 'Plan for Orderly Closure of Bradford Works', which was prepared by the UK management, reveals that the original planned closure date announcement was 1 May. The actual announcement was not made until some 12 weeks after the original date.

On 22 July, local MPs were told in strictest confidence that Bradford was to close. The following day, Bradford's 510 employees were told that their plant, which was operating at only 22 per cent capacity, would be closed and that all UK manufacturing would be consolidated at Doncaster.[36] Harvester's UK managing director explained that[37]

> Today ... is the formal notification of the redundancy which marks the commencement of the statutory 90-day period of consultation. Detailed discussion of the implementation of the closure will continue at plant level.
> The majority of the 510 people currently employed at Bradford will be leaving at the end of the 90-day period and beyond that date only a small run down team will be retained.

He added,[38]

> I can assure you that the Company really has done everything humanly possible to save Bradford and we should reflect on how much sooner they would have taken this decision, had it not been for their genuine regard for the plant.

Bradford was effectively closed on 22 October 1982. It was closed because Harvester could no longer retain more than one agricultural equipment plant in the UK. The largest plant was Wheatley Road, Doncaster, and it was physically possible to consolidate at that plant, whereas Bradford was too small for this to be possible.

Harvester's UK director of industrial relations during the early 1980s described the divestment process to me. Parent-company executives decided to close Bradford in February and informed senior UK management in late April, who in turn communicated the decision, within a day or two, to plant management.[39]

Senior UK management received the go-ahead from the US parent company to implement the closure in May/June, and only then was it empowered to inform employees. The UK management was very concerned that the closure of Bradford could provoke industrial action at its other plants in the UK, and was anxious to avoid any such action being taken. Had the employees taken industrial action, for example, production at Doncaster would have ground to a halt, with grave consequences for Harvester.[40]

A full-time union official told me that the Bradford work-force was divided and that relations were tense, indeed acrimonious, between staff and manual workers' unions. Attempts therefore to unite the two unions to form a joint committee to fight for the future of Bradford were unsuccessful. He believed that local management were 'messenger boys', devoid of decision-making powers, and that decisions even of minor importance were made at company headquarters in Chicago.[41]

Another union representative said that he believed that the divestment decision had been made long before employees heard of the company's proposals. He explained that local management had lost its credibility in the eyes of the stewards. He said that he did not believe the statements issued by management, and had eventually suggested to the UK director of industrial relations that perhaps the director was being deliberately misinformed by US management. The director replied that Harvester operated in an ever-changing market, that strategy and decisions were flexible, and that this factor accounted for any inconsistencies in company statements. He denied that management consciously misled shop stewards.[42]

Another shop steward told me that employees' representatives were 'reasonably well informed at most stages', although there was 'a great deal of room for improvement'. He added, 'I feel that the Company as a whole could not have cared less about the future lives of its employees and the effect of a closure as long as it got a trouble-free closure.'[43]

It would appear that plant closure always comes as a shock, even though events have indicated that it is inevitable. One union official admitted that the closure of Bradford proved a shock to him, even though he knew divestment was likely.

7.5 Caterpillar

Founded in 1925, the US MNC Caterpillar has risen to become the world leader in earth-moving equipment. With headquarters in Peoria, Illinois, it established its first foreign sales subsidiary in 1950. The UK was the chosen market, but production in the UK did not begin until 1956, when it acquired a former licensee, the Birtley Company Ltd, with its plant Birtley, near Newcastle, in north-east England. The same year saw the start of construction on a large new plant at Uddingston, near Glasgow, which came into operation in 1958.[44]

During the 1960s Caterpillar's expansion overseas continued, though by

Table 7.4   Performance data on Caterpillar Tractor Company, 1980–87

Year	Sales ($m)	Net income ($m)	Ave. no. of employees
1987	8180	350	54 463
1986	7321	76	53 731
1985	6725	198	53 616
1984	6576	(428)	61 624
1983	5424	(345)	58 402
1982	6469	(180)	73 249
1981	9154	579	83 455
1980	8598	565	86 350

Source: company annual reports

the end of the decade the industry had become much more competitive. In 1970 Caterpillar's president warned of the threat posed by Komatsu, the Japanese firm; but throughout the 1970s and beyond, Caterpillar remained leader in earth-moving equipment, its success due to superior management, a longstanding reputation for quality and a strong dealer network.

Favourable market conditions, plus Caterpillar's own competitive muscle, resulted in an exceptional year in 1981, with sales of $9.15 billion and profits of $579 million (see Table 7.4). That year remains the record year for both performance indicators.

At the start of the 1982 fiscal year there was thus little cause for pessimism in Peoria; but this soon changed. Sales were down a massive 29 per cent to $6.5 billion in 1982; worse still, Caterpillar suffered a loss—the first in fifty years—of $180 million. Between 1982 and 1984 Caterpillar's losses totalled $953 million. During this period, there was a disproportionate decline in sales outside the USA, which was largely due to the widespread cessation of major construction projects in debt-ridden developing countries.

The dramatic slump, which had been quite unexpected, demanded stringent measures if Caterpillar was to remain internationally competitive. Cut-backs in both capital investment and manpower were essential. Accordingly, 25 000 jobs were lost between 1981 and 1983. Worldwide employment, which had peaked at almost 90 000 in 1979, had shrunk to 58 000 by 1983. Similarly, capital expenditure was down by more than 60 per cent, from $836 million in 1981 to $324 million in 1983.

The situation facing Caterpillar worldwide had reached the critical stage, and a 22 per cent cost reduction programme was given top priority throughout the organization. Caterpillar had six plants in Europe: three in the UK (Birtley, Leicester and Uddingston), two in France and one in Belgium. Plant closures were necessary throughout the group. Several US sites were closed, as well as others in host nations. In 1983 the closure of

Birtley was announced. In early 1987, the company shocked Scotland with news of the closure of its Uddingston plant. In each case 1000 jobs were lost.

Birtley (Newcastle)

Background

As was noted earlier, Caterpillar acquired its plant at Birtley in 1956. This was a fabrication plant, while the more modern Uddingston factory was an assembly operation. Both operations were geared to the earth-moving equipment business, but Caterpillar's other UK factory, at Leicester, produced fork-lift trucks. In 1982, when rationalization of UK operations seemed highly likely, Leicester's future was not in question. The same could not be said for Birtley and Uddingston, where, already, production capacity had been run down. By January 1983 the number employed at both plants had been halved, but UK management asserted that there was no plan to close either operation.

Employee disclosure and consultation

In March 1980, short-time was introduced at Birtley. Local newspapers ran headlines announcing that production was being cut to avoid redundancies— 'Workers go on short time to save jobs'; 'Work cut to avert lay-offs'.[45] Local management issued reassuring statements to anxious employees who feared that they would be made redundant.

By late autumn 1981, trade union officials in Britain were concerned for their members at Caterpillar's UK operations. Redundancies, short-time working and repeated management statements of the slump in demand all served to underline the company's difficulties at parent and subsidiary level (see Tables 7.4 and 7.5).

Table 7.5 Performance data on Caterpillar Tractor Company Ltd, 1979–86

| Year | Sales (£'000) | Profit | | Ave. no. of employees |
		Before tax (£'000)	After tax (£'000)	
1986	235 432	2782	1012	1945
1985	171 278	(362)	(906)	1806
1984	155 190	1142	821	2248
1983	114 226	2865	3791	2608
1982	146 833	5493	6181	3703
1981	190 029	3914	11 871	5015
1980	208 978	(508)	94	5307
1979	183 258	5021	11 685	5288

Source: Extel Statistical Services

On 6 November 1981, at a trade union meeting specially convened to discuss Caterpillar, national delegates concluded that only parent-company management could provide them with relevant information; hence a meeting was sought with US management in order to determine investment plans.

Between March 1980 and January 1982, production at Birtley had been halved, and in June 1982 compulsory redundancies were announced at Glasgow. Shop stewards at the Scottish plant contacted their Newcastle counterparts, complaining that it was impossible to obtain a 'true picture' of the company's intentions.[46]

In January 1983 a three-day week was introduced at Birtley, where the work-force had already been almost halved in 18 months, from 2100 to 1100. Among those concerned for the plant's future was local Labour MP, Giles Radice. He had written on 1 December 1982 to Caterpillar's European vice-president, Pierre Guerindon, asking for a meeting to discuss the future of the Birtley plant. By 24 January, having not yet received a reply, he sent another letter bearing a similar request. He eventually received a reply from Mr Guerindon dated 5 January. In his reply, Mr Guerindon urged Mr Radice to speak to the Birtley plant manager:

> he can give you as much information as I can concerning the prevailing circumstances, and until some positive indication of a revival in business emerges, neither of us can be very helpful on the subject of future plans.

Six months later, in June 1983, full-time working was resumed at Birtley, after more than three years of short-time working; perhaps understandably, the work-force, concluded that their jobs were more secure. However, any such optimism was to prove ill-founded and short-lived.

On 15–17 August, senior parent-company executives gave presentations to financial institutions in San Francisco, Chicago and New York. The chief operating officer, Mr Gilmore, announced that the company 'was actively pursuing programs to reduce costs and improve employee/union relationships'. The former exercise, he said, 'would affect ... size and number of facilities'.[47]

Two weeks later, on 30 August, the industrial editor of Newcastle's newspaper, *The Journal*, discovered that on the following day Caterpillar would be announcing the closure of Birtley. He telephoned the chairman of the Shop Steward's Committee in the evening, asking him to comment on Caterpillar's decision to close the plant. The union official was astonished by this news, as was the work-force when they read of Caterpillar's decision in their newspaper the following morning.

On 31 August, the *Glasgow Herald* too was able to tell its readers that Newcastle was to close, and this was before any official company statement. (The Glasgow plant, meanwhile, had won a reprieve.)

Later in the day, Caterpillar announced its decision to close Birtley, but its failure to ensure that it was first to notify its employees did its reputation little good. On the other hand, it suggests that the journalists' actions merit consideration: given that they knew of the company's planned announcement, perhaps the journalists should have considered those affected and not pre-empted the company's statement.

After the closure announcement, several company–union meetings occurred prior to one on 14 October. At this meeting, the union delegation asked Caterpillar to delay the initial date of redundancies from 6 January to May 1984, and to improve its proposed terms of redundancy in the event of plant closure.

Caterpillar compromised, agreeing to delay the implementation of initial redundancies until 30 March and to improve the existing level of redundancy payments by 25 per cent, in return for employees' co-operation in the smooth shutdown of the plant by 31 August 1984. Four days later, at a mass meeting, employees voted to continue their opposition to the plant closure.

On 24 October 1983, the plant manager explained to shop stewards that Caterpillar's alternatives were as follows:[48]

(a) A phased and orderly closure which would be in the best interests of all concerned, with employees guaranteed employment to the end of March 1984 and with many going through to August 1984, all with decent severance payments; or
(b) An earlier plant closure which would really be in no one's interests.

Given the choice between imminent redundancy and the opportunity to work for a further six to nine months, plus having time to seek alternative employment and make the necessary emotional and financial readjustment, it was predictable, and understandable, that employees would choose the option that forestalled redundancy. Caterpillar knew that the stakes were too high for its Birtley employees. The work-force could not afford to gamble six to nine months' wages on testing the impact of the OECD's Guidelines on corporate decision-making—which is just as well, for only changing market conditions would have prompted Caterpillar to reverse its decision. Only one course of action was open to the Birtley work-force.

Within two days, employees agreed to accept a phased shutdown of the plant by 31 August 1984, but they exhorted their shop stewards to approach management once again for additional increases in severance pay. Exactly a week later, employees voted by 'a substantial majority to accept the phased shutdown of the plant by 31 August 1984, and the total severance package as now proposed by the Company'.[49]

It had taken six weeks for Caterpillar to break down opposition to closure, and a further two weeks to reach a settlement on redundancy payments. Therein lies the major problem facing union officials in the plant closure situation: the membership, for sound reasons, lacks confidence in its leaders' ability to persuade firms to reverse a major corporate decision. Thus, employees are likely to pressurize officials into early haggling over redundancy payments, so as to secure a good deal as early as possible after the closure announcement.

Caterpillar and the OECD Guidelines

On 30 September, the TUC announced that it was demanding an investigation 'under the OECD procedure' into the Birtley situation. It accused Caterpillar of a breach of the company's own code of conduct, the OECD's Guidelines and the Vredeling Proposals.[50]

According to Caterpillar's *Code of Worldwide Business Conduct and Operating Principles*, the company aspires to a 'high standard of human relationships' and intends 'to provide employees with timely information concerning company operations and results ... in which they logically have an interest'.[51]

In his letter to the OECD's UK national contact point, the then general secretary of the TUC expressed the view that the TUC 'is firmly of the view' that Caterpillar's actions 'constitute a breach of the Guidelines'. He identified paragraphs 6 and 9 of the 'Employment and industrial relations' section as 'the main areas of complaint'.[52]

By 9 November, Caterpillar had completed its response to the TUC's charges.[53] This document concentrates on 'three areas of particular interest': the economic background to the closure decision; employee disclosure and consultation; and the regulatory environment (i.e. UK law, OECD Guidelines and Vredeling). In the first section, Caterpillar cited cases of divestment by rival firms, in order to stress the difficult market conditions. As regards employee disclosure, the company indicated that employees and trade unions were 'fully informed' of these trends. According to Caterpillar's report,[54]

> By mid-August 1983, the UK Board had concluded that one plant in the UK Company would have to be closed ... it fell between Glasgow and Birtley Plants as to which should be considered for closing. Because Glasgow was already an assembly plant and a more modern facility, against the older and purely component manufacturing Birtley Plant, the conclusion was that Birtley should be closed. The intention to close Birtley was then ratified at a ... UK Board Meeting on 29 August 1983.

The company said that it had paid 'careful consideration' to its own code of conduct, the OECD's Guidelines and UK legislation in the timing of its closure announcement. It indicated that the closure announcement date had been brought forward because in Glasgow and Newcastle there had already been 'a great deal of speculation and rumour among employees that one of the plants would have to be closed'. Caterpillar also criticized the journalists responsible for pre-empting its closure announcements:[55]

> Unfortunately, some members of the press somehow learned of the planned announcement. To our regret, some portions of the media—although aware of the Company's intention to inform employees before making a public announcement—nevertheless published the news on the morning of 31 August.

On the question of UK legal requirements to provide 90 days' notice before issuing redundancy notices to 100 or more employees, Caterpillar announced the closure on 31 August 1983, but there were no compulsory redundancies until after 30 March 1984. Caterpillar therefore concluded that 'the period between initial consultation and implementation of redundancies amounted to seven months, 'or more than twice the period specified in the Employment Protection Act'. According to Caterpillar's code of conduct,[56]

> The law is a floor. Ethical business conduct should normally exist at a level well above the minimum required by law.

In reply to the TUC's specific charges that it had breached the OECD's Guidelines, especially paragraph 6 of the 'Employment and industrial relations' section, Caterpillar claimed it had 'complied entirely' with this section:[57]

> We communicated with employees and their union representatives well in advance of the proposed closure date.

In Chapter 3 above, it was seen that the OECD's national contact points are expressly forbidden to comment on the conduct of an individual enterprise; their function is to clarify, on request, sections of the Guidelines. Should a case arise in which a NCP is uncertain of the meaning of a particular section, the case is referred to CIME.

In his letter of 7 October 1983 to the UK national contact point, the general secretary of the TUC had stated that the TUC's main areas of complaint concerned paragraphs 6 and 9 of the 'Employment and industrial relations' section and paragraph 8 of the Introduction. He believed that,[58]

> taken together, these can be seen as calling for:
>
> timely consultations with union representatives before the announcement of such major changes as plant closures or other decisions with major effects of workers' livelihoods;
>
> opportunities for unions to negotiate on the issues with the management which has taken the decision;
>
> attempts to mitigate to the maximum extent practicable adverse effects from such decisions, again involving managements with authority to take the necessary decisions.

On 7 December, the UK national contact point, based at the Department of Trade and Industry, replied to this letter, disagreeing with the TUC's interpretation of the aforementioned sections of the Guidelines:[59]

> we would not accept that the Guidelines themselves provide for 'negotiation' on closure or transfer of undertakings.

In its reply to the TUC, the NCP did little more than summarize the document that it had received from Caterpillar. The TUC was disappointed that the NCP did not pass judgement on Caterpillar, and this would suggest that the TUC still has not come to grips with the strictly defined, and limited, roles of the OECD's NCPs and CIME. The Caterpillar Birtley experience has led the Economic and Social Committee of the TUC to the following conclusion:[60]

Overall ... it confirms ... the inadequacy of voluntary codes of conduct, and the need for statutory rights to information and consultation such as those in the draft Vredeling proposals. ...

Uddingston (Glasgow)

Background

In 1985 Caterpillar's profits were less than in 1972. As world demand fell, competition became even more intense as firms fought for orders to take up the slack in their manufacturing facilities. A price war was being waged in Europe. Caterpillar's arch rival, Komatsu of Japan, had been selling machines for 30 per cent less in Europe than in Japan where they were produced. Eventually, in 1985, the European Commission responded to allegations of 'dumping', and imposed a 26.6 per cent tariff on Komatsu's earth-moving equipment. The Japanese firm overcame this barrier by establishing its first manufacturing operation within the EC: it acquired from the local council the former Caterpillar plant at Birtley, Newcastle.

The closure of Birtley in 1984 should have served as a constant reminder that Uddingston occupied a humble position in Caterpillar's global strategy. But three years later, rather than announce the closure of the Scottish plant too, Caterpillar had decided that Uddingston would play a crucial role in its global strategy. The US corporation had decided to commit $1 billion to revolutionize the manufacturing process at its 30 plants worldwide. This investment programme was labelled 'Plant With a Future' (PWAF)—owing to the fact that, without such investment, many of Caterpillar's plants faced closure. The objective was to reduce manufacturing costs by at least 15 per cent, in order to eradicate Komatsu's cost advantage. PWAF is co-ordinated by a head office group of 300.

On 18 September 1986, the 1200 employees at Uddingston, most of whom were members of the Amalgamated Engineering Union (AEU) (previously the AEUW), were told that the Scottish plant would receive a massive injection of £62.5 million. The very same day, a few miles away in Glasgow city centre, Gavin Laird, the general secretary of this union, told his audience at a conference on 'Scotland and the Multinationals: New Developments and Future Prospects' that the idea of international trade union solidarity was a romantic myth. Ironically, then, when the Caterpillar workers at Uddingston were battling to save their plant, the Scottish Trades Union Congress called on the support of Caterpillar workers in France and Belgium.

The day after this announcement, the Scottish secretary of state, Malcolm Rifkind, attended the plant to hear the American plant manager inform the media of Caterpillar's proposed investment. On the 20 September a 'family day' was held at the plant. A Caterpillar video presentation heralded 'Glasgow's Role in the Company's Global Scheme for the 1990s and Beyond into the Next Century'.[61]

In order to appreciate the rationale for Caterpillar's closure announcement 16 weeks later, it is perhaps useful to recall the broader financial environment of the autumn of 1986. My own view is that the Uddingston closure was in response to Caterpillar's fears that it might be taken over. In late September, $800 million was knocked off Caterpillar's market value as the company's share price fell from $46 to $38. In the autumn of 1986, merger mania swept the USA; the decline in Caterpillar's market capitalization presented an ideal opportunity for another company or corporate raiders to mount a takeover bid.

Caterpillar had certainly been aware of such a threat, and the Illinois-based company had only recently been reincorporated in the state of Delaware, whose legislation favours the target in a takeover bid. The chairman and president's message to shareholders in the company's *Annual Report 1985* referred to the threat of 'unsolicited takeover attempts' and urged shareholders to accept new charters and bylaw provisions, or 'poison pills', to ward off predators.[62]

Fears that Caterpillar could become the subject of a hostile takeover bid no doubt mounted when, by mid-October, it became apparent that Goodyear was 'in play'. Shortly afterwards, Goodyear received a hostile $5 billion bid from Sir James Goldsmith. At the same time, Gillette, the world market leader in razors, was on the receiving end of a hostile bid. In order to raise its share price and maximize shareholders' returns, thereby discouraging a hostile bid, Caterpillar, like many other corporations, erected its first defence by implementing tough rationalization programmes which led to closures and job cuts.

Employee disclosure and consultation

In September Uddingston plant manager, Ken Robinson, had announced that 'the £62 million can be looked upon as insurance against the loss of 1200 jobs'. The secretary of state described Caterpillar's investment as 'absolutely marvellous news for engineering and for jobs in Scotland'.[63]

In November 1986, Ken Robinson remained convinced that Caterpillar was committed to his factory. As guest lecturer at a Strathclyde International Business Unit seminar, he proudly told his audience of MBA students that the £62.5 million investment safeguarded Uddingston and the 1200 jobs there. In the December issue of *Caterpillar Earthmover*, the in-plant newspaper, his message to the work-force was one of optimism and commendation of employees' 'positive achievements'.

On 3 January 1987, in his 'New Year Message', Mr Rifkind again paid tribute to Caterpillar as a company that had 'become more profitable and competitive, so helping to make employment more secure'. Eleven days later, on 14 January, Caterpillar announced its decision to close Uddingston. The disclosure followed days of speculation following a newspaper report on 10 January which read: 'Caterpillar ... is expected to announce in the next few weeks that it is shutting some of its 30 manufacturing plants around the world'.[64]

Plant management stated that, while no decision had been taken, a company statement was imminent. Like the Birtley work-force, employees at Uddingston had to rely on the media rather than the company to first alert them to the possibility of closure. Unlike their counterparts in England, however, the Scottish workers instantly took direct action in an attempt to reverse the company's decision. On the day that closure was announced, the workers occupied the factory; the sit-in lasted 103 days, ending on 27 April. Uddingston closed on 4 November 1987.[65]

Employees' condemnation of a divestment decision is to be expected, but Caterpillar also riled the Scottish secretary of state, who described the company's decision as 'deplorable and inexplicable'. He was shocked and enraged by the company reneging on its plans to invest £62 million in Uddingston, and by its failure to consult the work-force. His sentiments were echoed by every political party in Scotland. The financial contributions of the population of central Scotland to the 'Support the Caterpillar Workers' fund was testimony to the public's sympathy for the employees and dismay at the US corporation's conduct.

7.6 Conclusions

At their peak, the four plants examined in this chapter each employed more than 2000 workers. By the time closure was announced, the work-force at each had been significantly reduced, especially at Birtley and Bradford. All three MNCs received strong criticism from trade union officials, but this chapter reveals that it was not always deserved. Massey-Ferguson kept its work-force fully aware of its problems and the implications for its Kilmarnock plant. At the other extreme, from a public relations perspective, Caterpillar bungled the Birtley divestment, gaining notoriety for its somewhat shabby treatment of its employees. Three years later, it appeared that the MNC had learned nothing from the Birtley experience, and once again its name was mud.

Foreign divestment theory

The four plant closures examined here tend to support Boddewyn's contention that an eclectic theory of foreign divestment seems much more appropriate than the mutually exclusive condition-, motivation- and precipitating-circumstance-based theories. Apart from Caterpillar Uddingston, the closures were initially triggered by the exceptionally dramatic downturn in the agricultural and earth-moving equipment industry. This slump, along with record high interest rates, represented a significant change in market conditions from the postwar boom period during which all four plants had been acquired or established.

By the late 1970s, the industry was operating at well below full capacity and firms were unable to achieve satisfactory economies of scale. There can be no question that the slump was rapid and unexpected. In 1976 Massey-Ferguson reported record profits, and in 1977 it launched a £2 million investment programme at its Ayrshire plant. But just four years later, only a Chrysler-style bail-out saved the Canadian MNC from bankruptcy. Similarly, Harvester enjoyed record sales and profits in 1979, but two years later it too tottered on the verge of bankruptcy. Caterpillar was another victim of the sudden slump. In 1981 its sales and profits peaked, but the following year it suffered its first loss in fifty years.

Thus, all three MNCs had strong motivation to rationalize global operations, particularly those in developed countries. The extent of retrenchment can be seen in the number of jobs lost at each firm since 1979. In that year the worldwide employment level of each firm was as follows: Caterpillar 90 000, Harvester 98 000 and Massey 56 000. In 1987 the figures were: Caterpillar 54 000, Harvester (i.e. Navistar International) 15 000 and Massey (i.e. Varity Corporation) 18 969.

The closure of the Glasgow plant may also have been due to market conditions, but the author has argued that the main motive was Caterpillar's takeover defence tactics. When stock markets take a short-term perspective, corporate strategists must deliver immediate benefits to shareholders. The PWAF programme entailing investment in Uddingston was a long-term project which ran contrary to the climate on Wall Street in the autumn of 1986. Thus, a short-term solution had to be found to reduce Caterpillar's production costs. By closing three plants, including Uddingston, the company's excess capacity problem was immediately ameliorated. None of the four closures was due to the plant's poor performances. For different reasons, each firm had to rationalize its operations worldwide.

Both the Massey and the Harvester cases testify to the importance of overcoming 'barriers to exit' in the divestment process, and the precipitating-circumstance-based theory. Massey was apparently willing, in order to save 500 jobs, to undertake the expensive option of transferring baler production from Marquette rather than close Kilmarnock. Similarly, according to a UK spokesman, the closure of Bradford was postponed simply because the factory was held in such high regard within the corporation. However, local managers can prove 'barriers to exit', and representatives from the home country are often sent to oversee divestment in the host country. This was the case with Harvester. In February 1982 the British chairman of Harvester UK resigned unexpectedly, just 14 weeks after his appointment. His resignation appears to have coincided with the Chicago headquarters' decision to close Bradford reaching senior UK subsidiary management. Significantly, he was replaced by an American, whose loyalties were clearly to the parent company rather than to the UK subsidiary.

Managerial literature stresses the likelihood of divestment following the arrival of new men who have no emotional attachment to any particular division or unit and therefore have no 'barriers to exit' to overcome. The Black–Rice leadership was barely a month old when Massey announced its Feasibility Study on European combine production. Similarly, Harvester had a regular turnover in chief executive officers. These boardroom reshuffles are symptomatic of an ailing company, as is the jettisoning of loss-making operations.

Employee disclosure and consultation

Massey's UK management claims it was heavily involved in the divestment decision, but, as was seen earlier, the final decision rested entirely with the president, British-born Victor Rice. Before reaching his final decision, he himself flew from Canada to Britain to meet union officials, who were given an opportunity to argue the case for retaining combine production at Kilmarnock. Union leaders were therefore given access to the real decision-maker.

The decision made, employees were informed as soon as minimum preparations for disclosing the fact had been completed. Kilmarnock was closed 98 days later. The Canadian MNC went to great lengths to find a buyer for the plant, and it established Moorfield Manufacturing, which would initially provide employment for 54 of the Kilmarnock employees.

Similarly, Harvester's decision to close Bradford was made at head office in the home country. The planned date for announcing Bradford's closure was originally 1 May 1982; however, the announcement was postponed until 23 July. Virtually all employees were made redundant on 22 October. They had received 90 days' notice, the absolute legal minimum.

News of the divestment decision had been communicated to UK management by February 1982 at the latest, and senior subsidiary management began preparing for closure, but for five months at least UK management withheld from employees the firm's intention to close the Bradford plant. In other words, management withheld news of the closure for five months, while it gave the 550-strong work-force only three months' redundancy notice.

It therefore seems reasonable to conclude that Harvester failed to consult trade union representatives 'at the earliest possible opportunity', as stipulated in the 1975 Employment Protection Act. However, the Department of Employment itself regards this term as being of 'minor significance where the redundancy involves 10 or more employees'. It can be concluded that, while Harvester conformed to UK legislation—it did give 90 days' notice—UK management consciously misled the work-force in order to restrict organized resistance to closure.

Harvester's UK management argued that a firm's conduct should not be gauged simply by the length of the redundancy notification period. They cited the Caterpillar case to substantiate their argument. Caterpillar employees first heard of the company's decision to close the Birtley plant on the local radio, yet it was a year later that the factory closed. Harvester's senior UK executives believe that, although they gave less notice of closure, they have a more positive attitude to employee disclosure and consultation—a claim that does not seem unwarranted.

It has to be remembered that, at the time of the Bradford closure, International Harvester was in the throes of crisis and, unlike Caterpillar, could not afford a gradual rundown, which would only imperil jobs at other plants. UK management and union officials held regular discussions, and a considerable amount of information was disclosed to these employees' representatives—indeed, to the work-force itself. On the other hand, union officials were denied access to the real decision-makers, who alone were capable of reversing the divestment decision—the parent-company executives.

Caterpillar maintained that UK management was involved in the Birtley divestment decision-making process. This claim was greeted with scepticism among trade union officials, and the company's subsequent conduct at Uddingston suggests that their reaction was not ill-founded. In both closures, the media alerted Caterpillar's employees to the threat of closure; in the Birtley case, journalists actually informed the work-force.

Caterpillar's behaviour suggests that the company's own code of conduct serves little purpose other than as a useful public relations tool. In both closures, Caterpillar exceeded the notification requirements of the Employment Protection Act. Little wonder, therefore, that European trade unions have campaigned for more extensive legislation on employee disclosure and consultation. Similarly, the lack of consultation with employees at Birtley and Uddingston perhaps shows why Caterpillar was so opposed to the EEC's Vredeling Proposals.

The Caterpillar closures confirm the limited—if not negligible—value of the OECD's Guidelines in influencing corporate behaviour. Caterpillar remains the only foreign MNC which the TUC has accused of violating the Guidelines in the course of the foreign divestment process. The TUC's decision to refer the corporation to the OECD's UK national contact point is open to two interpretations: either the TUC had failed to appreciate the futility of this exercise because of the rules surrounding administration of the Guidelines, or it simply used the referral for publicity purposes. Whatever the reason, it is significant that the TUC chose not to invoke the Guidelines in its efforts to avert the closure of Uddingston.

Four closures involving three MNCs were examined in this chapter. Only Massey-Ferguson can justly claim to have held meaningful consultations with employees' representatives. Yet even this MNC has been subject to severe criticism from academics and former employees. It appears that, regardless of the reasons for foreign divestment or the firm's endeavours to act with due regard to the interests of stakeholders, any MNC closing a plant is in a no-win situation and is regarded by the work-force as callous and greedy.

Such blanket criticism may tend to serve only to dissuade firms from good conduct and increase the likelihood of their meeting just the minimum legal requirements, rather than seeking a more magnamimous solution.

References

1. Director of administration, Caterpillar Tractor Co., letter of 4 December 1980 to Dr G. Adam, member of European Parliament.
2. D. Lea, assistant general secretary of the Trades Union Confederation, letter of 12 January 1984 to Arthur Scott, district secretary for Tyne and Wear of the Confederation of Shipbuilders and Engineering Unions.
3. Caterpillar, *Century of Change*, May 1984, p. 58.
4. Caterpillar, 'Synopsis of Remarks by L. L. Morgan, Chairman and Chief Executive Officer, R. E. Gilmore, President and Chief Operating Officer, E. J. Schlegal, Executive Vice-President', 15–17 August 1983.
5. Massey-Ferguson, statement to employees, 8 September 1978.
6. A. Dawe, director of communications Europe, Massey-Ferguson, letter of 11 April 1985 to author.
7. Massey-Ferguson, press statement, 7 November 1978.
8. Massey-Ferguson, press statement, 16 May 1979.
9. Thomas, Kilmarnock factory director, 'Statement Made to All Bargaining Units at Kilmarnock', 9 October 1979.
10. 'Massey plant braced for total closure', *Glasgow Herald*, 31 October 1979.
11. H. Hebden, managing director of Massey-Ferguson's UK subsidiary, 'Massey-Ferguson cease operations at Kilmarnock', press statement, 9 November 1979.
12. A. Dawe, director of communications Europe, Massey-Ferguson, letter of 2 November 1984 to author.
13. W. Woods, interview with author.
14. Ibid.
15. Ibid.
16. Ibid.
17. Ibid.
18. Ibid.
19. Ibid.
20. Baldry *et al.*, 'Multinational capital in Scotland and the closure of the Massey-Ferguson plant, Kilmarnock', unpublished paper, University of Strathclyde, Glasgow, Scotland.
21. A. Dawe, director of communications Europe, Massey-Ferguson, and J. Thomas, Kilmarnock factory director, interview with author, 12 December 1984.
22. Ibid.
23. International Harvester, *Harvester Facts*, February 1984.
24. Ibid.
25. 'At Caterpillar, both sides may bend', *Business Week*, 15 August 1983, pp. 54–8.
26. International Harvester, *Annual Report*, 1981.
27. *Business Week*, op. cit.
28. International Harvester, 'Notes of SCJNC Meeting Held at Bradford on 16 May 1980'.
29. 'Final sad end to Harvesters', *Telegraph and Argus*, 18 October 1982.

30. International Harvester, 'Notes of Extended SCJNC and M2–M6 Held on 5th November 1980 at Doncaster'.
31. International Harvester, 'Notes of Extended SCJNC Meeting Held on March 11 1981'.
32. International Harvester, 'Notes of Joint CJNC, SCJNE, M2–M6 Meeting Held on 25th June 1981'.
33. 'Slump blamed for IH Job Cuts', *Telegraph and Argus*, 9 January 1982.
34. 'Harvester jobs get county lifeline', *Telegraph and Argus*, 11 March 1982.
35. 'Firm slams jobs report', *Telegraph and Argus*, 12 March 1982.
36. International Harvester, press release, 23 July 1982.
37. International Harvester, statement to CJNC, 23 July 1982.
38. Ibid.
39. I. Page, director of industrial relations, International Harvester (Great Britain), interview with author on 11 September 1984.
40. Ibid.
41. J. Jefferey, Regional Officer for ASTMS (MSF), telephone interview with the author on 31 August 1984.
42. W. Coultard, chairman of the Joint Negotiating Committee, telephone interview with author, August 1984.
43. Ms Husarz, chairman of APEX at Bradford plant, letter of July 1984 to author.
44. Caterpillar, May 1984, op. cit.
45. 'Workers go on short time to save jobs', *Gateshead Post*, 3 April 1980; and 'Work cut to avert lay offs', *The Journal*, 28 March 1980.
46. Negotiating Committee Notebook, Birtley, June 1982.
47. Caterpillar, 15–17 August 1983, op. cit.
48. Caterpillar, 'Summary of Events Concerning the Closure of the Caterpillar Birtley (Newcastle) Plant (Summary)', November 1983.
49. Ibid.
50. Trades Union Congress, Dunlop and Caterpillar press statement, 29 September 1983.
51. Caterpillar, *Code of Worldwide Business Conduct and Operating Principles*, 1974.
52. L. Murray, general secretary of the TUC, letter of 7 October 1983 to C. Batten, UK National Contact Point for the OECD's Committee on International Investment and Multinational Enterprises.
53. Caterpillar, 'Shock as boss quits firm', *Telegraph and Argus*, 24 February 1982.
54. Ibid.
55. Ibid.
56. Caterpillar, 1974, op. cit.
57. Caterpillar, November 1983, op. cit.
58. Murray, op. cit.
59. C. Batten, letter of 7 December 1983 to L. Murray (see no. 52 for further details).
60. TUC Economic Committee, internal document, 1984.
61. J. Foster and C. Woolfson, *Track Record*, Verso Books, London, 1988.
62. Caterpillar, *Annual Report 1985*.
63. Foster and Woolfson, op. cit.
64. *Financial Times*, 10 January 1988.
65. Foster and Woolfson, op. cit.

8
Summary and conclusions

The main objective of this book has been to illustrate by detailed analysis the foreign divestment process of multinational corporations in the UK context, with particular reference to employee disclosure and consultation. The book may help corporate executives, employees' representatives and policy-makers to achieve their objectives *vis à vis* foreign divestment, and may make some contribution to the development of foreign divestment theory. It allows for an evaluation of the effect of UK legislation on foreign MNCs regarding employee disclosure and consultation, and tries to shed some light on the Vredeling debate.

8.1 Foreign divestment theory

It has been said that closures of foreign-owned plants in the UK have been due mainly to certain unfavourable changes in the business environment. The rising cost of oil, foreign competition, high interest rates, market saturation and social and technological change created strong motives to divest; for the UK—indeed, Europe—no longer held the location-specific advantages that had prompted the original investment.

As these adverse changes took their toll on the companies, new chief executives were appointed to mastermind recovery. It must be stressed, however, that the need for rationalization had already been triggered by one or more of the variables in Table 8.1, and the arrival of a new man at a troubled firm should have been seen as a signal of intention to divest, rather than as a cause of divestment.

No company appears to have closed a plant simply because of a perceived opportunity to make larger profits elsewhere, although MNCs often face this very charge. Overall, there can be little doubt that the closures examined here were considered necessary by the parent company in order to safeguard its market share and profitability, which had already been heavily undermined by intense competition.

Given the current wave of merger activity, it is worth stressing that a number of large foreign-owned plant closures in the UK were due to post-acquisition restructuring (e.g. Nabisco Huyton; Peugeot Linwood).

Identifying the exact cause of the Caterpillar Uddingston closure has proved problematic, but it has been suggested that it was not unconnected to a corporate defence against a possible hostile takeover bid.

Table 8.1 Adverse changes in the business environment and the divestment of foreign plants in the UK

Divestment factor	Foreign-owned plant*													
	1	*2*	*3*	*4*	*5*	*6*	*7*	*8*	*9*	*10*	*11*	*12*	*13*	*14*
Emergence or increase in competition from:														
Japan and the East			×	×		×		×	×	×			×	×
Western Europe					×	×		×	×	×				
Eastern Europe					×	×		×	×	×				
the US	×	×												
Recessionary conditions	×	×	×		×	×	×	×	×	×	×	×	×	
Record high interest rates											×	×	×	
Soaring raw material costs	×	×												
Social change			×			×		×	×	×				
Technological change reducing product life-span, and leading to obsolescence of plant and equipment						×		×	×	×				
Takeover defence mechanism														×**

*1 = Monsanto, Dundonald
 2 = Akzo Antrim
 3 = Singer, Clydebank
 4 = Grundig, Dunmurry
 5 = Hoover, Perivale
 6 = Goodyear, Drumchapel
 7 = Goodyear, Craigavon
 8 = Firestone, Brentford
 9 = Firestone, Wrexham
10 = Michelin, Mallusk
11 = Massey Ferguson, Kilmarnock
12 = International Harvester, Bradford
13 = Caterpillar, Birtley
14 = Caterpillar, Uddingston
**Caterpillar has never suggested that the decision to close Uddingston was a response to merger-mania in the US, but the author argues in Chapter 7 that the surprise decision may have been part of the corporation's takeover defence strategy.

8.2 The foreign divestment decision and employee disclosure and consultation

This study confirms that the foreign divestment decision is invariably taken by the parent company, though in some cases UK subsidiary management claimed to have been involved in the decision-making process (e.g. Caterpillar Birtley; Michelin).

In two instances (i.e. Goodyear Craigavon and International Harvester), the case studies reveal a time-gap in relaying information of the foreign divestment decision to employees, who were not informed for some months after the decision had been taken at US headquarters.

Of the 14 closures, in only 5 (Akzo, Singer, Hoover, Goodyear Drumchapel and Massey-Ferguson) were employees given any formal indication by plant/national/parent-company management that closure was possible; however, in many cases employees strongly suspected that closure was likely, often despite repeated assurances from plant/national management that their jobs were secure. Only 3 of the 14 closures could be described as unexpected: 2 in Northern Ireland, involving Grundig and Michelin, and Caterpillar in Scotland. In contrast, two MNCs (Akzo and Goodyear) delayed divesting because they appreciated the grave economic and social impact that their decision would have on the regions affected.

The cases illustrate that multinational corporations can resort to various strategies in the foreign divestment and employee disclosure situation. Whichever is chosen, the company is subject to criticism from employees; but careful planning can allow the MNC to withdraw with its image intact. The corporation that divests unexpectedly (e.g. Michelin), and appears to pay scant regard to local sensitivities (e.g. Caterpillar) can expect a hostile reaction not only from the work-force, but also from the media, civic groups and the host-country government.

Having appraised corporate conduct, it is worth noting that the behaviour of the work-forces at Goodyear Drumchapel and Singer was such that their employers could have been forgiven for concluding that a closure decision would not be unpopular. In most cases, however, the work-force explored every channel to retain their plant, and on at least one occasion this ironically included arguing that an alternative UK plant should be closed.

Employees' representatives, too, must recognize the importance of public relations. They may choose to pursue a certain course of action on principle, despite corporate warnings of the consequences. Abandoning that course when the multinational stands by its ultimatum is merely inviting condemnation for irresponsible behaviour.

8.3 The regulatory environment and the OECD's Guidelines for Multinationals

In the UK, companies proposing 100 or more simultaneous redundancies at the same plant must give employees' representatives at least 90 days' notice. Of the 11 firms featured in the case studies, 4 (Caterpillar, Hoover, Michelin and Singer) gave significantly longer notice. Nevertheless, union officials were very critical of these MNCs. For example, Michelin was denounced in the Northern Ireland Assembly; in the Birtley case, Caterpillar was condemned in the European Parliament and was reported to the OECD for breach of the

Guidelines for Multinational Enterprises; while in Glasgow the Caterpillar work-force staged a lengthy 'sit-in', during which they produced an earth-moving machine which they hoped to donate to the Third World.

In Chapter 3, the value of the OECD's Guidelines was questioned, and their application in the Caterpillar Birtley case reinforces this verdict. The key section of the Guidelines, the 'Employment and industrial relations' chapter, merely exhorts companies to abide by national legislation, and should not be construed as a supplement to national laws. Given this, it is hardly surprising that so many managers and union officials were unfamiliar with them.

With regard to the European Community's Vredeling Proposals, the revised text lacks precision, but it is difficult to imagine that it could confer any significant benefits or advantages to labour. The EC's Mass Dismissals Directive has been enacted by member-governments. The UK, like other EC countries, requires employers to consult employees' representatives when redundancies are proposed. The evidence presented here suggests that firms notify employees and hold consultations only when it has already been decided to issue redundancies.

The 1975 Employment Protection Act, which arose from the EC's Mass Dismissals Directive, has proved unsuccessful in ensuring, first, that workers receive maximum notification of redundancies, and second, that every opportunity is given them to present their views before a final decision is reached. In practice, regulators have not been concerned that companies do not hold these aims. Instead, they have been satisfied simply to establish the floor level of notice that employees must receive.

Despite focusing on a negative aspect of inward investment, namely foreign *divestment*, the message to emerge from this study is that Britain—and Europe too—may have lost its location-specific advantages for some investors, but for many more it remains a highly desirable location, Foreign divestment will continue, but delays in restructuring may prove counter-productive. Protracted debate and discussion on further employee disclosure and consultation legislation has tended to divert attention away from more pressing matters.

Selected bibliography

Aharoni, Y., *The Foreign Investment Decision Process*, Harvard Business School Division of Research, Cambridge, Mass. 1966.

Bane, W. T. and F. F. Neubauer, 'Diversification and the failure of new Foreign Activities', *Strategic Management Journal*, **2**, 3, 219–33, July–September 1981.

Blanpain, R., *OECD Guidelines for MNEs and Labour Relations 1976–79*, Kluwer, Deventer, 1979.

— *The OECD Guidelines for Multinational Enterprises and Labour Relations: Experience and Mid-Term Report 1979–1982*, Kluwer, Deventer, 1983.

— et al., *The Vredeling Proposal, Information and Consultation of Employees in Multinational Enterprises*, Kluwer, Deventer, 1983.

Bluestone, B. and B. Harrison, *The Deindustrialisation of America*, Basic Books, New York, 1982.

Boddewyn, J. J., 'Divestment: local vs. foreign and US vs. European approaches', *Management International Review*, **1**, 21–27, 1979.

— 'Foreign divestment: magnitude factors', *Journal of International Business Studies*, **10**, 1, 21–27, Spring–Summer 1979.

— 'The theory of foreign direct divestment: a first pass', Paper to Eastern Regional Annual Meetings of Academy of International Business at New York University, April 1981.

— 'Notes on a theory of foreign divestment', a paper presented at the annual meeting of the academy of management, Dallas TX, August 1983.

— 'Foreign and domestic divestment and investment decisions: like or unlike?', *Journal of International Business Studies*, **14**, 1983.

— 'Foreign direct divestment theory: is it the reverse of FDI theory', *Weltwirtschaftliches Archiv*, 119, 345–55, 1983.

— and R. L. Torneden, 'The divestment decision process', *Academy of Management Review*, 1979.

Broke, M. and G. Turner, 'Why managers don't dispose', *Management Today*, pp. 84–148, May 1971.

Buckley, P. J. and P. Enderwick, *The Industrial Relations Practice of Foreign-Owned Firms in Britain*, Macmillan, London, 1985.

Business International, *International Divestment: A Survey of Corporate Experience*, New York, 1976.

Campbell, D. C. and R. L. Rowan, *Multinational Enterprises and the OECD Industrial Relations Guidelines*, The Wharton School, University of Pennsylvania Press, Philadelphia, 1983.

Casson, M. (ed), *The Growth of International Business*, Allen and Unwin, London, 1983.

— *Multinational Enterprises and World Trade*, Allen and Unwin, London, 1986.

— *The Firm and The Market*, Blackwell, Oxford, 1987.

Caterpillar, *A Code of Worldwide Business Conduct and Operating Principles*, 1974.

— *Century of Change*, May 1984.

Chopra, J., J. J. Boddewyn and R. L. Torneden, 'US foreign divestment: A 1972–75 updating', *Columbia Journal of World Business*, **13**, 14–18, Spring 1978.

Dicken, P., *Global Shift: Industrial Change in a Turbulent World*, Harper and Row, London, 1986.

— *International Production and the Multinational Enterprise*, Allen and Unwin, London, 1981.

— *Multinational Enterprises, Economic Structure and International Competitiveness*, Wiley, Chichester, 1985.

— *Japanese Participation in British Industry*, Croom Helm, London, 1986.

Foster, J. and C. Woolfson, *Track Record*, Verso, London, 1988.

Gray, S. J., *Information Disclosure and the Multinational Corporations*, Wiley, Chichester, 1984.

Gray, S. J. and M. C. McDermott, 'International mergers and takeovers: a review of trends and recent developments', *European Management Journal*, **6**, 1, 26–43, Spring 1988.

— 'International Mergers: The Pursuit of Global Market Leadership', 15th Annual Conference, European Association for Research in Industrial Economics, Rotterdam, 31 August–2 September 1988.

Grunberg, L., *Failed Multinational Ventures: The Political Economy of International Divestments*, Lexington Books, D. C. Heath, Lexington, 1981.

Hamilton, G., *The Vredeling Proposal and multinational trade unionism*, Centre for Multinational Studies, Washington, September 1983.

— 'The control of multinationals: what future for international codes of conduct in the 1980s', *IRM Multinational Reports*, No. 2, October–December 1984.

— 'How to market a divestment', *McKinsey Quarterly*, pp. 52–59, Summer 1973.

Hood, N. and J. E. Valhne (eds), *Strategies in Global Competition*, Croom Helm, London, 1987.

Hood, N. and S. Young, 'US Investment in Scotland: Aspects of the Branch Factory Syndrome', *Scottish Journal of Political Economy*, (3), 279–294, 1976.

— *Multinationals in Retreat: The Scottish Experience*, Edinburgh University Press, 1982.

— *Multinational Investment Strategies in the British Isles. A Study of MNEs in the Assisted Areas and in the Republic of Ireland,* HMSO, London, 1983.
— *Industry, Policy and the Scottish Economy,* Edinburgh University Press, 1984.
Hout, T., M. E. Porter and E. Rudden, 'How global companies win out', *Harvard Business Review,* 98–102, September–October, 1982.
International Labour Office, *Tripartite Declaration of Principles regarding MNCs and Social Policy,* 1977.
Kitching, J., *Acquisitions in Europe: Causes of Corporate Successes and Failures,* Business International, Geneva, 1973.
McDermott, M., *'Singer, Clydebank: anatomy of closure',* undergraduate dissertation, University of Glasgow, 1982.
— *Foreign Divestment and Employee Disclosure and Consultation in the UK, 1978–85,* doctoral thesis, University of Glasgow, 1988.
OECD, *International Investment and Multinational Enterprises, Guidelines for Multinational Enterprises,* Paris, 1976 (revised 1979).
— *International Investment and Multinational Enterprises, Review of the 1976 Declaration and Decisions,* Paris, 1979.
— *International Investment and Multinational Enterprises, Mid-Term Report on the 1976 Declaration and Decisions,* Paris, 1982.
— *International Investment and Multinational Enterprises, Review of the 1976 Declaration and Decisions,* Paris, 1984.
Porter, M. E., 'Please note the location of nearest exit—exit barriers and planning', *California Management Review,* 21–33, Winter 1976.
— 'Changing patterns of international competition', *California Management Review,* **28** (2), 9–39, 1986.
— *Competition in Global Industries,* Harvard Business School Press, Boston, Mass., 1987.
Robinson, J., *Multinationals and Political Control,* Gower, Aldershot, 1983.
Sachdev, J. C., *A Framework for the Planning of Disinvestment Policies of Multinational Companies,* Doctoral thesis, UMIST, Manchester, 1976.
Spanhel, C. L. and J. J. Boddewyn, 'The crisis divestment decision process: a descriptive model', February 1983 mimeo (paper was also presented at the Annual Meeting of the Academy of Management, New York City, August 1982).
Spanhel, C. L. and D. Johnson, 'Issues in the study of US foreign divestment: a review of major studies', paper presented at the Annual Meeting of the Midwest Academy of International Business, Chicago, 1982.
Van den Bulcke, D. in *Handbook of International Trade,* (eds. M. Z. Brooke and P. J. Buckley), Kluwer, London, 1982.
— et al., *Investment and Divestment Policies and Multinational Corporations in Europe,* Gower, Aldershot, 1979.
Stopford, J. M. and L. Turner, *Britain and the Multinationals,* Wiley, Chichester, 1985.

United Nations Centre on Transnational Corporations, *Transnational Corporations in World Development: Trends and Prospects*, United Nations, New York, 1988.

Wilson, B. D., *Disinvestment of Foreign Subsidiaries*, UMI Research Press, Ann Arbor, 1980.

Young, S., N. Hood and J. Hamill, *Decision-Making in Foreign-Owned Multinational Subsidiaries in the United Kingdom*, ILO Working Paper No. 35, International Labour Office, Geneva, 1985.

— *Foreign Multinationals and the British Economy*, Croom Helm, London, 1988.

Index